Faith Confronts Nuclear Power

Faith Confronts Nuclear Power

A THEOLOGICAL CRITIQUE

JOHN R. GUGEL

Foreword by Edward H. Schroeder

RESOURCE *Publications* · Eugene, Oregon

FAITH CONFRONTS NUCLEAR POWER
A Theological Critique

Resource Publication
An Imprint of Wipf and Stock Publishers
199 W. 8th Ave., Suite 3
Eugene, OR 97401

www.wipfandstock.com

ISBN 13: 978-1-4982-1870-2

Manufactured in the U.S.A.   10/06/2015

Dedication

I met Kay Drey while I was studying for the ministry at a Seminary in St. Louis. It was a most improbable relationship that has grown into a friendship spanning half a century. At the time, Kay was committed to achieving racial diversity within her community, University City, Missouri.

Together we founded the organization known as "New Neighbors," later changed to "County Open Housing." Her interests have expanded to include a fierce desire to bring an end to nuclear power. She led the fight for the defeat of the Callaway Nuclear Power Plant and succeeded in stopping the construction of a second nuclear reactor on the site. Her wish to bring an end to this dangerous and outmoded source of energy knows no limit. She brings to the task passion and humor. I could not have written this without her support.

Contents

Table and Illustrations

Foreword

In the very opening chapters of the Bible—strictly speaking, the Hebrew Scriptures—the tempter teases our primal parents with this pitch: "Look, you can be like God. And that's a good idea. So try this." And so they do, even though the creator had said this was a no-no and the consequences would be lethal. Their offspring have followed their example ever since.

In ancient Greece, there was a parallel story. Prometheus (literally "fore-thinker," possibly even rendered "someone who thinks for himself") challenges Zeus's omnipotence, invades Olympus to steal the divine fire, and winds up suffering forever.

Other cultures share similar ancient legends. And lethal it always is. Every such attempt brings catastrophe for the human agents who attempt to go over the line into the divine. A few chapters later in the Bible comes a repeat performance of what happened in Eden. It is the Tower of Babel human creatures seeking to literally move into the creator's turf to occupy the creator's chair and thereby, of course, move the creator out.

The scholarly term for such narratives is "mythos"—mythos in the classical Greek meaning of that term: not a fictitious story, but a "true" story, a parable that exposes a deep truth of human life through a storyline that permeates the whole human race. In this case, the human yen—insane though it always is—is to *not* be content with being "merely" creatures of the creator, but to usurp the creator's turf and take it over on their own. (Better said, on "our" own. For I am implicated in this as well.)

John Gugel reports here on one such Promethean attempt in our own time. Namely, using atomic energy to fabricate here on earth the "fire" that burns in the sun—not mythological Prometheus, but *us*. Or, in Biblical imagery, to replicate for the umpteenth time the Tower of Babel story as "our" story. And, of course, as said the Ur-tempter, it is not really wickedness to be such forethinkers. *Au contraire*, for "good" will come from that trans-gression. That's been the tempter's promise from the get-go.

But to "be like God" is trans-gression—literally, going over the boundary. This transgression is ultimately lethal for a bound-ary-jumper whose existential structure is to be a creature of God, an "image" of the deity but not a deity per se. Humans are not "wired" to be deities. You might say: We imitate the image of God through the technology of "divine" electrical circuitry. But only at twelve volts. We're not wired for the deity's 240—or possibly 24000 volts. Every attempt to plug into the deity's circuitry has but one consequence: Burn, baby, burn.

"Babel" is the name used in the Hebrew Bible for the city of Babylon. Babel is also the Bible's diagnostic term for human would-be invaders of God's turf. Regardless of their country of ori-gin, they are "Babylonians." In John Gugel's lifetime (mine too) the Babylonian heart is still among us—actually still in all of us—and still at work in tower-construction. John's book is about possibly the tallest such tower: atomic energy, which attempts to replicate the sun's action down here on earth.

I remember attending a conference years ago sponsored by ITEST, the Institute for Theological Encounter with Science and Technology, just as atomic energy was coming over the horizon. Both atomic physicists and theologians were in attendance. I've never forgotten the words of one of the scientists: "I'm all in favor of atomic energy, just so long as the plant is ninety-three million miles away from where I live. Planet earth can't handle what goes on in the sun."

Foreword

Was that a scientist's way of telling the Tower of Babel story today? I thought so.

Are there more towers now under construction? Genetically modified organisms? Stem-cell stuff? Genome repair? Fracking? All of the above projects come with proposed benefits for human life on earth. But is Promethean trans-gression occurring in, with, and under these projects as well? Are our Babylonian hearts building another tower?

At the very least, that question needs to be asked. Granted, it may not be easy to get a clear answer. But it needs to be pursued. Not "for God's sake"! Nor for the sake of theologians like John Gugel, but for *our* sake. For the sake of human life on this planet, human survival—the ostensible "good for human welfare" that each projects' proponents proclaim. For if it is a trans-gression, or crossing the line into the divine, then we must consider that the track record from time immemorial is self-destruction. Not because God is mean and punishes intruders, but because no human being is wired to run on God's voltage. To attempt such a trans-gression is not merely stupid, but ultimately suicidal.

Granted, it often takes a long time before the results are in. A thousand years are like a day and vice versa—not only in the creator's time-keeping, but in that of creation too. For the same drip-drip-drip that creates the Colorado River has, after a zillion years, created the Grand Canyon.

John Gugel is not merely asking the question "Is atomic energy on earth trans-gression?" He says it is. He puts before our eyes vivid, even grisly, evidence of the self-destruction already underway. He may be a "voice crying in the wilderness" (John 1:23), and there may indeed be pushback, but that's not a bad label for John Gugel to have. In Christian history, the first person so designated was God's agent (Biblical Greek actually calls him an "angel") to be a whistleblower for folks in his time. The issue then, as now, was self-destruction. A cousin of that "angel" later said to the same audience: "Father, forgive them, for they know not what they do" (Luke 23:34).

Foreword

The name of that ancient whistleblower was John, the same name as the author of this book. Hmmm!

Yes, none of that is good news. *Au contraire*. Humans going over the line into the divine always wind up being bad news. The good news in the Christian story comes with its own *au contraire*, when the divine goes over the line to enter our turf—to become human—and does so not with divine fire, but with a still small voice, initially heard from a babe in a manger. Like the first whistleblower John, our second whistleblower John weaves the good news story of the mangered Messiah into his bad news narrative. Good for him! Good for us!

Rev. Dr. Edward H. Schroeder
St. Louis, Missouri

xii

Acknowledgments

My appreciation goes to my family: my dear wife, Linda, who has stood by me through my debilitating life with Parkinson's; my grown children, Jeremy, Jessica and Nathan; and to my delightful grandchildren, Jackson Isaiah, Grace Elizabeth, and Adrian Kwan, who love and accept me no matter what shape I'm in. My prayer is that my grandchildren will inherit this earth better than we found it.

My thanks go to my assistant, Jennifer Lynch, who was helpful in so many ways; the staff and residents of Brookdale Place; my sister-in-law, Liz Behring, for her help with footnotes; Mary Ann Merz, PhD, MPH, whose editing skills made my rather prosaic prose sing; my friend and supporter, Mark Aamot; Ed Schroeder, whose encouragement was invaluable; Frank Waltz, whose fresh insight into the manuscript was quite helpful; Heidi Bischmann, who made the design for the cover; and finally, to Flora, my assistance dog, whose companionship I value so much.

Nuclear Power's Dirty Secret[1]

If a massive asteroid hit the Earth, ending human life as we know it,
would it make a difference that we had been here?

—Derek Parfit, philosopher

I remember the Vice President for Nuclear Systems of Iowa Power Company telling me that he would not be worried living next door to a nuclear power plant.[2] I wonder if he took into account the facts reported in the following essay by Kay Drey, reprinted here with her permission:

Nuclear Power's Dirty Secret
by Kay Drey

Want to know the best-kept secret about nuclear power plants?

1. Drey, "Nuclear Power's Dirty Secret." Reprinted from an essay first published in *Viewpoint: A Forum on Energy and Environmental Issues*, 1990, Safe Energy Communications Council.

2. Lloyd Siever, mayor of Altoona, Iowa, in a personal interview with the author.

It doesn't take a Chernobyl meltdown for a nuclear power plant to release dangerous radioactivity into our air and water. All it takes is the plant's everyday, routine operation.

Nuclear power plants can't operate without regular, deliberate releases of radioactive water and gases. The releases from the reactor building are needed to control the pressure, temperature, and humidity, and to keep radioactivity from exceeding government limits for workers.

Think of water boiling in a kettle. The escape of steam relieves pressure inside. A nuclear power plant operates in much the same way; hot, radioactive gases inside the reactor building must be vented into the atmosphere. This is done through vents that are built into the building. The vents have filters to stop some of the radioactive gases from being released. However, no filtering technology exists for some gases, like xenon-135, which decays into cesium-135, an isotope with a three-million-year half-life.

The kettle analogy also helps explain routine releases of radioactivity into the river, lake or ocean that supplies a reactor's cooling water. As the water in the kettle boils, minerals build up on the interior. Likewise, radioactive corrosion products stick to the interior surfaces of the reactor vessel. Some of this radioactive "crud" as it is called, sloughs off into the reactor's cooling water. Fission products also enter the cooling water from leaks in the fuel rods, which contain the equivalent long-lived radioactivity of 1,000 Hiroshima bombs.

How does this contaminated water make its way into the environment? Given the maze of more than 50 miles of piping through which cooling water circulates, leaks are bound to occur. In fact, the Nuclear Regulatory Commission allows leaks of up to 10 gallons a minute. And as a nuclear plant ages, the leaks generally increase.

Some contaminated water is intentionally removed from the reactor to reduce the level of radioactive and corrosive chemicals that damages valves and pipes. This radioactive water is "cleaned up" and either recycled back into the cooling system or released into the environment.

As with the plant's gases, not all radioactive isotopes can be filtered from water. No economically feasible technology exists to do so. Tritium, or radioactive hydrogen, for example, cannot be filtered. Just as water containing ordinary hydrogen and oxygen is a component of all living cells, tritiated water, a major byproduct of nuclear power plant operation, can also be incorporated into all the cells of the body. Many laboratory studies have shown that long-term chronic exposure to low concentrations of tritium is more damaging than previously believed. Some of the hazards resulting from tritium uptake include mutations, tumors and cell death.

Other radioactive isotopes are also released without being filtered when they are at a concentration below the level the plant monitors are set to detect—a level the government has decreed "acceptable." But "acceptable" doesn't mean safe: It means "as low as reasonably achievable." In other words, as low as the industry claims it can afford to achieve.

So, no one really knows how much radioactivity is released.

The nuclear industry and the Nuclear Regulatory Commission say we should not be concerned about these routine releases. But in a report published in December 1989, a National Research Council committee of radiation experts states that well-demonstrated health effects from low-level radiation "include the induction of cancer, genetically determined ill-health, developmental abnormalities, and some degenerative diseases."

In a June 1990 statement recommending more stringent radiation exposure limits for workers, the International Commission of Radiological Protection says: "New data and new interpretation of earlier information now indicate with reasonable certainty that the risks associated with ionizing radiation are about three times higher than they were estimated to be a decade ago." In addition, Dr. John Gofman, who co-discovered uranium-233 and founded the Biomedical Research Division of the Lawrence Livermore Laboratory, states in his most recent report on low-dose radiation that there is no such thing as a "safe dose" of radiation, and that a low dose received slowly causes as many cancers as the same dose delivered all at once.

The nuclear industry often justifies its routine releases of radioactivity by asserting that humans are constantly exposed to natural background radiation that has nothing to do with nuclear weapons or power plants. However, while we cannot lower the level of natural radiation, no one has the right to add manmade radiation on top of it. Any exposure to radiation increases the risk of genetic mutations, cancer, and other life-shortening diseases. The short-term benefits of nuclear-generated electricity do not justify the possible long-term consequences of radiation exposure.

Nuclear power plants don't have to blow up or melt down to release radioactive poisons into our air and water. All it takes is their routine, everyday operation. Government and industry have known this for decades. It's time the public knew it, too.

Introduction

"What is your book about?" people would ask me when they found out about this project. I would watch their eyes glaze over as I attempted to explain the reach of this book, something that to my knowledge had never been attempted before: namely, a theological examination of nuclear power to critique this method of electrical generation through the eyes of faith.

It is my hope that reading this book will lead you to a deeper understanding of the threat posed by nuclear power and a new commitment to its abolition. As a result of my study of this topic, I found nuclear power to be full of promise in the beginning of the Nuclear Age but one that has since proven to be dangerous and deadly, threatening life itself on our planet. For this reason, I believe that nuclear power is a failed technology and should be eliminated as a source of energy.

It is my hope that this slim volume will serve as a wake-up call to action. We are one disaster away from the next catastrophic meltdown of a nuclear reactor. Whether by human error or natural causes (including earthquake, tsunami, flood, hurricane, and fire), we can't predict how this may happen.

1

Welcome to Fortunate Island

Radiation is frightening, but there is life beyond it. I won't let it limit me; I won't let a power plant take my life away.

—Mari Kobayashi, Fukushima Daiichi survivor[1]

The worst thing that can happen to a nuclear reactor—a meltdown and explosion—happened at the Fukushima Daiichi power plant in Japan on March 11, 2011. The catastrophic accident occurred when one of the five worst earthquakes in the history of the world struck the island nation. It was followed closely by a massive tsunami that swept away human bodies, schools, hospitals, and manufacturing plants—taking with it twenty thousand lives. The quake registered 9.0 on the Richter scale.

Several days later, first one, then another, and finally three of six nuclear reactors exploded and caught fire. The tsunami easily topped the thirty-three-foot-high seawall built to protect the

1. Osnos, "Fallout," 17.

1

six-reactor campus. Suddenly, Fukushima Daiichi was on the map. Ironically, the name Fukushima Daiichi is translated as "Fortunate Island." The terror visited upon the people of that prefecture could be described as anything but fortunate.

Today, there remains a twelve-mile vacancy limit around Fukushima. Absolutely nothing may be brought into the imposed vacancy zone. No agriculture, no housing, no planting—nothing productive may be built within twelve miles of the burned-out buildings. The US State Department has warned American citizens to stay at least fifty miles away from the plant and to defer travel to Japan.[2] American scientists estimated that the Fukushima Daiichi reactors leaked an astonishing 365 times the acceptable amount of radiation into the air at the site of the explosion.[3]

Some of the heaviest concentrations of the fallout were in the village of Iitate (population 6,200), twenty-five miles northwest of the plant. Less than a year earlier, it had been named one of "Japan's 100 Most Beautiful Villages."[4] Residents were given an official order to evacuate at the end of May, two months after the earthquake: "When the oldest man in town—a hundred and two years old—heard the news, he committed suicide rather than flee ... In front of the village's town hall, a machine that looked like an oversized parking meter flashed a real-time radiation reading in large red digits ... Being there was equivalent to receiving a chest x-ray every twelve hours."[5]

Long before the explosion, some unknown people had erected a sign that now seemed to mock the survivors. It declared, "Nuclear Power Is the Energy of a Bright Tomorrow."[6]

Japan's love affair with the atom did not occur overnight. First, the Japanese public would need to be sold on the efficacy of nuclear power. World War II came to a halt with the atomic bombing of Hiroshima and Nagasaki. After such an experience,

2. Ibid., 7.
3. Ibid.
4. Hoviss, "Iitate Village," 19.
5. Osnos, "Fallout," 7.
6. Ibid., 3.

one would think the Japanese would be skittish about all things nuclear.[7] Japan, however, relies on innovation to make up for the country's lack of natural resources. The Japanese needed to find another source for electricity since they lacked both coal and oil. Nuclear power was viewed as the necessary supplier of the electricity needed to power industry.

Workers are especially vulnerable to the risks of nuclear power. One group of laborers at the Fukushima plant, called "nuclear gypsies," was among the low-level workers who roam from reactor to reactor looking for employment. "At the time of the tsunami, some of the workers at the Fukushima Daiichi plant were earning the yen equivalent of eleven dollars an hour—the same as part-time help at McDonald's were paid in Tokyo."[8] They were on the lowest rungs of the ladder. In the West, they would have been called "jumpers"—nuclear workers willing to jump in and jump out of high-dose conditions.

Vocabulary for the Nuclear Age

The Nuclear Age has given us a unique vocabulary, to say the least. Such a vocabulary relies on understatement to label even a piece of the nuclear pie. Indeed, it takes understatement to a new low. "Nuke Speak," we might call it.

Nuke Speak	Definition
Event, Accident, Episode, Incident	Catastrophic meltdown of a nuclear power plant.
Gray Unit	Amount of radiation absorbed by the body in a nuclear "event."
Acceptable and Permissible	Not necessarily safe, but rather as low as reasonably possible from a cost-benefit analysis.
Uprating	Allowing reactors to run hotter and faster.

7. Ibid., 2.
8. Ibid., 7.

Jumper	A nuclear worker willing to jump in and out of high-dose conditions. (Also known as "gamma sponges," "dose fodder," and "glow boys.")
High-level Waste	The radioactive material resulting from spent nuclear fuel reprocessing, including radioactive materials that require permanent isolation.
Low-level Waste	Everything else.
Swimming Pool	A place for "temporary" storage of high-level waste containing water.
CRUD	Chalk River Unidentified Deposits.
Seismic Event	Earthquake.
Yellow Cake	Uranium after milling.

Lest we think it couldn't happen in the United States, on August 23, 2011, just five months after the earthquake in Japan, a 5.8 magnitude earthquake followed by a hurricane struck the eastern coast of the United States, with Virginia at its epicenter. The largest quake in the area in more than a century, it affected twenty American nuclear reactors, most seriously the North Anna plant in Virginia. There, the ground shook with greater intensity than the plant was designed to withstand: "Concrete containers of spent fuel that weighed a hundred and seventeen tons shifted a few inches. Five days later, when Hurricane Irene struck the East Coast, emergency sirens failed to function properly at three nuclear plants, and at Indian Point a canal overflowed. On September 9th, Nuclear Regulatory Commission (NRC) staff people suggested ordering power plants to review their ability to survive quakes and floods 'without unnecessary delay.'"[9]

This was not the first time the United States had been threated with nuclear disaster. In 1979 there was a meltdown at the Three Mile Island nuclear power plant in Pennsylvania, just eleven miles from the state capital, Harrisburg. The meltdown was triggered by a mechanical failure followed by a series of automatic events and

9. Ibid., 11.

human misinterpretations that caused the reactor core of 100 tons of uranium to overheat and melt. Unfavorable weather conditions trapped the radioactive emissions that escaped from the plant. Neither the nuclear industry nor the US government collected release estimates for specific isotopes or measured how much radiation was released.[10]

The Nuclear Regulatory Commission (NRC) of the United States is charged with protecting public health and safety. It provides oversight for the safety of nuclear reactors and materials, waste management, and issues license renewals. There are ninety-nine nuclear reactors currently operating in the United States. By the end of 2014, five will have been shut down (Vermont Yankee in Vermont; San Onofre's Units 2 and 3 in California; Kewaunee in Wisconsin; and Crystal River in Florida), presumably forever. Alarmingly, the NRC has approved twenty-year extensions of the operating licenses for seventy-three of the existing nuclear power plants. Besides permitting these plants to operate beyond their forty-year design, the NRC also granted permission for them to run hotter and faster. Investigative journalist Karl Grossman, along with activists from organizations such as the Sierra Club and the Coalition Against Nukes, view such decisions as inviting catastrophe and call for nuclear power to be replaced by safe, clean energy technologies such as wind and solar power.[11]

It became clear on Fortunate Island that we, as a human race, particularly in the plundering economies of the northern countries—the so-called first world—have heavy work to do and serious choices to make if we are to pass on a livable world to our children and to all the children of the world. Critical decisions and urgent choices have been put off for far too long.[12] "If we do not solve our collective pollution/energy problem together, then we will all suffer together."[13]

---

10. Caldicott, *Nuclear Power*, 65–66.

11. Grossman, "License to Kill," 1.

12. Osnos, "Fallout," 5.

13. Shuster, *Beyond Fossil Fools*, 104.

The God of Creation has given us a useful paradigm in the first three chapters of the Hebrew Scriptures—a call to action we must answer if we are to help ourselves out of the colossal mess in which we find ourselves. An in-depth examination of that ancient document's rich meaning is called for. The times in which we live might be likened to the primordial stew that existed when God "in the beginning" started the creation process rolling.

2

God Is Creator of All That Exists[1]

God writes the Gospel not in the Bible alone, but also on trees, and in the flowers and clouds and stars.

—Martin Luther[2]

We worship a God who is known as the Creator of all existence. The creation story is told primarily in two accounts that represent two separate strands within the Hebrew Scriptures. These two strands are quite different stories with different points of view.[3]

The first story, known to scholars as the "P," or priestly account, comes to us from God's faithful people of the Babylonian exile. In the P version of the story, God speaks, and a whole

---

1. aka The Old Testament
2. *The Green Bible*, I-103.
3. Borg, *Reading the Bible Again*, 63.

universe comes into being. This is in contrast with the "J," or Yahwist, account.

In the J story, God kneels in the dust and forms the first human by hand, then breathes life into him CPR-style. In the P account, you find none of this hands-on style of creating. God speaks, and it is so. God's hands, according to P, do not get dirty. God is depicted as remote. In Babylon, the gods had too many human characteristics, so the author avoided any kind of anthropomorphism or ascribing human characteristics to God.

The P account is the better-known version of the creation story. The language is poetic and liturgical. Of particular importance is P's focus on the creation of humanity. We are told that humans are created in the "image of God" (Gen 1:27).

Both creation stories make it abundantly clear that human life is a gift. The psalmist wrote that human life is precious. As it comes to us from the hands of a loving God, life is priceless: "God has crowned [human beings] with glory and honor" (Ps 8:5).

The capture of the descendants of Israel by the Babylonian Empire was the pivotal event leading to the composition of the first creation story. Every human being is worthy of being held in honor and respect and of living in community with God and other human beings.

We need to remind ourselves of that fact because of the imminent threat to human life poised by nuclear power. The Creator gives human beings the capacity to think for themselves and to make decisions for the whole creation. In return, God invites joyful noise from all the earth, as in the following verse: "Make a joyful noise to God, all the earth; sing to him the glories of his name; give to him glorious praise" (Ps 66:1–2).

On Panama's Gulf coast there is a church called Iglesias de Santo Felipe, popularly called Church of the Black Christ. Over the years, birds too many to number have built nests on the beams and fly through the air as if the church were an aviary. The cacophony of sound these birds make as they join together, chirping and chattering, in glorious praise of their creator.

God made all things and declared them good. God continues to show love and care for creation throughout human history. At the beginning of the biblical narrative, God creates the heavens and the earth. God sweeps over the void and brings about light and life, declaring it very good.

In a world where terrorists, with little regard for human life, have caused havoc and brought unspeakable tragedy into the lives of innocent people, it may seem like darkness is overtaking the planet. But over and against that terrifying threat sounds the word of God, echoing over the deep and murky waters with "Let there be light" (Gen 1:3). And behold, there is light—and the darkness cannot ever overcome it! We have God's creative, eternal, incarnate Word on that.

Here we gain an idea of how pre-scientific people understood the world. They did not know that the sky stretched to the edge of the universe billions of light years away. Rather, they understood the sky to be a rigid dome—a gigantic inverted bowl: "Let there be lights in the dome of the sky to separate the day from night; and let them be for signs and for seasons and for days and years; and let them be lights in the dome of the sky to give light upon the earth" (Gen 1:14–15).

In the Bible, water is seen as a gift from God for its life-giving power. God often uses water to deliver his people, as at the Red Sea. Here the waters from the primordial deep are separated in another reference to God's taking charge of the pre-existing chaos.

To consider these accounts as scientific or historical fact is to ask the wrong question. In fact, they are the observations of "science" in the sixth century BCE. Neither the P account nor the other prominent version of the creation story, the J account, claims to be a book of science or a history book. Neither account answers the questions of *when* or *how*, nor should we expect that of them. They do answer the questions of *why* and *what*. Why did God create this world, and what are we doing with and to it? This is the most important question because the answer reveals God as the loving, merciful being who created this marvelous world for us to inhabit. Their purpose is to impart theological truth; they tell us something about God, namely that our God is good and gracious.

When the exiles were in Babylon, there was an overwhelming, all-embracing darkness to their existence. The first thing God says is, "Let there be light" (Gen 1:3). And behold, there was light! "And God separated the light from the darkness" (Gen 1:4). God is depicted as the light-giver known to the exiles as the one who would ultimately deliver them from bondage. In *Luther's Small Catechism*, Martin Luther professed his belief in God the Creator. Luther wrote this in 1522 CE as a summary of the meaning of the first article of the Apostles Creed:

An Article of Faith

I believe that God has created me together with all creatures. God has given me and still preserves my body and soul: eyes, ears, and all limbs and senses; reason and all mental faculties. In addition, God daily and abundantly provides shoes and clothing, food and drink, house and home, spouse and children, fields, livestock, and all property—along with all the necessities and nourishment for this body and life. God protects against all danger and shields and preserves me from all evil. God does all this purely out of [parental] and divine goodness and mercy without any merit or worthiness of mine at all! For all this I owe it to God to thank and praise, serve and obey [God]. This is most certainly true.

—Martin Luther[4]

Human Life Is Precious

The creation stories' descriptions of human beings make it abundantly clear that human life is precious. Life comes to us from a loving God. We were created in the "image of God" (Gen 1:27),

4. SC II 2.

which means that every human being deserves to be held in the highest honor and respect.

When we look at the world—this world that God created—we must mourn for how we have spoiled it. As a human race, we face difficult choices, even terrifying and urgent choices. The window of opportunity is rapidly closing. The choices we face now are lousy because we have made poor choices in the past. We have chosen consumption over conservation, production over prudence, exploitation over sharing, selfishness over community, and wastefulness over thrift. We have depleted the Earth of its natural treasures—we have poisoned its streams, spoiled its soil, plundered its forests, fouled its air, and ruined its atmosphere.

One of this lifetime's most poignant experiences is touring the National Holocaust Museum in Washington, DC, or its counterpart in Los Angeles. To see the evidence of the massive horror and cruelty unleashed by one group of human beings against another defies one's sense of humanity. Such barbaric torture and murder of a whole population is unfathomable. And the fact that these atrocities took place in a country as "civilized" as Germany, with all its rich culture, music, and literature, should give us all pause.

During the Holocaust, we saw the depths of depravity we human beings can fall to when we fail to respect, honor, and cherish human life. Since then, the world has witnessed the regime of terror of Idi Amin Dada in Uganda, "ethnic cleansing" in Bosnia, the Hutu's slaughter of the Tutsis in Rwanda, and the reign of terror of Pol Pot in Cambodia, to name only a few.

Each of us bears the image of God: "Then the Lord God formed man from the dust of the ground and breathed into his nostrils the breath of life; and the man became a living being" (Gen 2:7–8).

We ought to do all that we can to exalt, enhance, enable, embolden, and energize human life. The Scriptures link God's creating activity to God's justice, as in the following passage:

> Happy are those whose help is the God of Jacob, whose
> hope is in Yahweh their God, who made heaven and

earth, the sea, and all that is in them; who keeps faith forever; who executes justice for the oppressed; who gives food to the hungry. (Ps 146:5–7)

The Whole of God's Creation

The sun, moon, and stars are not identified by name in the first creation story. The author leaves them nameless so there is no confusion with the religion of the Babylonians, who worshipped those heavenly objects as gods. Only the Creator—not the objects of the Creator's work—is to be worshipped. The sun, moon, and stars are not presented as fearsome deities whose favor is to be curried through sacrifice and whose wrath is to be avoided at all costs, as ancient peoples thought.

God blesses what God creates. "Be fruitful and multiply" (Gen 1:22), God tells the creatures. It is God's creative intention that they fill the universe he made; that they grow, reproduce, and flourish; and that their motion and flight, whether frolicking in the deep blue seas or soaring high aloft, might be doxologies—songs of praise—to the God who called them into being. In this way, they serve God. And the fact that God blesses them makes clear that all God's creatures are important.

In the "greening" of the planet—the creation of grass and grains and great green forests of fruit trees and giant evergreens—all good things were given to us and to all humankind from the hand of a gracious God. Perhaps we might all be more conscientious in our care of nature if we remembered that it is the priceless, irreplaceable gift from our loving Creator. Nature does not belong to a privileged few; it was created for the benefit of all.

One cannot help but feel awe when contemplating the mysteries of eternity, of life, and the marvelous structure of reality. It is enough if one merely tries to comprehend a little of this mystery every day.

Clearly, the Bible makes a strong claim that the God of Israel is the Creator of the world. At the same time, the Bible makes no attempt to make that claim as a scientific statement.

We read that God "formed" the human. The original Hebrew word is often used to describe the work of a potter. What a beautiful image that creates in our mind of a potter at work. She skillfully and lovingly shapes the wet clay with patient hands until she is satisfied with her creation. In the process, she gets her hands mighty dirty. The prophet Jeremiah also employs this analogy to describe the relationship between Israel and God in Jer 18:6, where God says, "Just like the clay in the potter's hand, so are you in my hand, O house of Israel."

God shifts gears from potter to grand landscaper as he plants a garden and fills it with wonderful trees! The trees are both lovely to the eye and bear delicious fruit for we humans to eat. Two trees are singled out and identified. These are the "tree of life" and the "tree of the knowledge of good and evil" (Gen 2:9). Both trees will play major roles in the drama that is about to unfold.

The name of "the tree of the knowledge of good and evil" has particular significance in that the Hebrew concept of knowledge means more than mere accumulation of facts—it also involves participation in that which is known. So to know good and evil is to actively participate in both.

The verdant area surrounding the Tigris, Euphrates, and Nile rivers (which flow through modern-day Iraq and Ethiopia) roughly corresponds to the territory Israel controlled outright under King David or indirectly through strategic alliances. The theological point is that the rich bounty of God is the source of the empire's existence. This understanding comes with the explicit warning that what God gives, God can also take away if God's people are not faithful.

The Tower of Babel account in Gen 11 does not conclude with a gracious deliverance of any kind. Rather, the people are scattered and rendered incapable of communicating with each other.

God gives humans a purpose for being, and that is to work. Every worthy vocation contains within it the opportunity to serve

God. We often speak of our work as our "calling." The word "vocation" comes from the Latin *vocare*, which means "to call." Martin Luther would label this "ministry." When we work, we are carrying out God's intentions for the world. We participate in God's ongoing creative activity. We are making the world function.

Martin Luther's insight that the garbage collector who does his job well fulfills his calling just as completely as any bishop moves us to practice justice, show kindness, and do good to others as we go about our daily tasks. Now we see those tasks as God-given privileges and responsibilities and not just as a means of making a living. So it was that when a Roman Catholic church in St. Louis redecorated its sanctuary, it commissioned an artist to paint a large mural depicting people in such diverse vocations as a police officer, postal worker, firefighter, nurse, and priest as a way of lifting up and celebrating the many ministries to which God calls his people.

The Story of Adam and Eve

The Adam and Eve story begins with a story of creation. The Yahwist includes this story so as to compare the pristine beauty of the garden of Eden before the first sin (Gen 2) with the horrible condition of the world afterwards (Gen 3). This part of the story contains taut dialogue, tension, pathos, finely drawn characters, a touch of humor, irony, and a universal theme. What more could you ask of a drama?

It begins with a Hebrew pun. The Hebrew words *arumin*, meaning "naked," and *arum*, meaning "crafty," are derived from the same Hebrew root. The Yahwist uses this play on words to forge a connection between the wholesome, pristine world of Gen 2 and the disastrous loss of innocent paradise in Gen 3.

Up to this point, the first man and the woman have lived in a state of moral innocence. They have no sense of shame, for they have nothing to be ashamed of! This little pun sets the stage, foreshadowing that something grave is about to enter the picture.

Next, the Yahwist introduces a new character to the story. The author uses a serpent for good reason. One of the themes the Yahwist develops throughout Gen 2 and continuing through the book of Numbers is Yahweh's uncompromising opposition to the Baal fertility cults.[5] Throughout their history, the people of Israel succumbed to the appeal of these cults, often forsaking God altogether in their embrace of their next-door neighbors' religion.

Now, at the pinnacle of Israel's success as a nation under David, the Yahwist sensed the ground shifting in that direction once again. As a labor of love, the Yahwist wrote this extensive story of God's loving actions towards God's people to warn them to be faithful to Yahweh and not be swept away by the allures of the Baal fertility cults. What was God up against? What was these cults' appeal?

The agrarian society in which most everyone lived in that time depended on timely and adequate rain and good weather. The fertility cults promised to deliver both. In that sense, the Baal fertility cults are not all that different from those of our own day. Cults then and now promise wealth, success, and power.

In place of Baal, we sacrifice much of our lives on the altar of hard work in our climb up the corporate ladder. Today's fertility cults have a name; we know them in our time as an illness or addiction called "affluenza." For now, let's summarize affluenza this way: We go through life committing ourselves to consumerism's fertility cults only to discover at life's end that we have been worshipping the wrong gods. The fact is that prosperity and affluence do not deliver the things we really need in life. They might quench our thirst for more—if only for the moment. Having acquired the one thing we feel we need the most, we soon go on to the next longed-for "goody." Martin Luther taught that our god is that to which we commit our lives.

---

5. For more on the Baal fertility cults in connection to the Babylonian exile, see *New World Encyclopedia*, s.v. "Baal," http://www.newworldencyclopedia.org/p/index.php?title=Baal&oldid=989811, last modified August 5, 2015.

The Yahwist warns God's people of the very real danger they faced. The serpent played an important role in the worship life of the Baal fertility cults. By introducing the serpent as the tempter in this story, the Yahwist makes clear the dangers of affluence and complacency.

The Yahwist gives the cults their due; they are beguiling. The serpent is crafty. It has done its homework and believes it has spotted the chink in the armor—the place where the humans are vulnerable.

The serpent approaches the woman and draws her into conversation. Did the serpent target her specifically? Did it hide in the trees and bushes until it could catch her alone? Or did she just happen to be in the wrong spot at the wrong time? Would the serpent have pressed its case differently with the man? It doesn't matter. This is what matters: the serpent offers equality with God, and the humans jump at the beguiling offer. The serpent accuses God of holding back on the couple.

The serpent catches the woman's attention by misquoting God. God's actual words in Gen 2:17 were "Of the tree of the knowledge of good and evil you shall not eat," but the serpent asks the woman, "Did God say, 'You shall not eat from any tree?'" (Gen 3:3). This is a blatant ruse to hook the woman, and it gets a response.

The serpent is not disappointed. What exactly is the serpent after? We will soon find out. The serpent wants to estrange humans from God. The woman answers the serpent, telling it that if they eat of the tree in the middle of the garden, they will die.

The serpent practically roars back, "Call God's bluff. You won't die. Trust me!" Then, the serpent appeals to the worst instincts we humans share by asking, "Why is God keeping this from you?" The serpent is sowing seeds of mistrust and is about to reap a great harvest. "If you eat this, God knows what you will be like . . . you will be God!"

The basic human instinct is to want to be in control. This episode raises a critical question for our lives: What issues are calling us to mistrust God?

Eve saw:

1. That the tree was good for food (as if there wasn't enough food already at their disposal),

2. That the fruit was a delight to the eyes (as if the garden was not beautiful enough), and

3. That the tree's fruit could make them wise (as if these humans did not know all that they needed to know).

She took of its fruit and ate. See how her lack of trust in God completely distorted her vision? What are the things that distort our vision? What blocks our line of sight so that we no longer see the multitudinous grace of God toward us?

Suddenly, innocence was lost. For the first time, humans experience shame. They knew instantly that something was wrong, so what did they do? They quickly sewed fig leaves to cover themselves, to somehow cover their guilt and hide the naked truth about themselves. What happens when we cross boundaries? What happened when the president of the United States crossed a boundary with a young White House intern? He tried to cover it up, bringing an impeachment upon himself and disturbing the whole country with a shameful trial. The first consequence of crossing boundaries is that we feel shame and suffer a falling out with ourselves.

Next, the couple heard God walking. It was time to face the music. God's footsteps were drawing closer. So what did they do? They tried to hide. Their shame goes much deeper than having their bodies exposed. They are ashamed because they have been unmasked. The truth is out about them, and the more they try to hide, the more they engage in denial, and the worse it becomes for them.

Humans had been created to live in harmony with God, with one another, and with the whole of creation. The garden that had been a place of such sheer beauty and delight now becomes a hiding place—and not a very good one at that. What we see here is a mirror reflection of our own lives. When we cross boundaries—when we sin—the second consequence is that we fall out with God. "I hid because I was naked," was the humans' lame excuse.

"Who told you that you were naked?" (Gen 3:11). Or, in other words, "Did you do the unthinkable?" God wants to know.

And what does the man do? He blames the woman and—in a bit of primeval *chutzpah* — he blames God as well, essentially saying, "Remember who gave the woman to me, God. I was doing fine before she came along." When we cross boundaries, we fall out first with ourselves, second with God, and third with those closest to us.

"What about you?" God asks the woman. "What is your story?" (Gen 3:13). God hands down his judgment in reverse order. Yahweh dispenses with the serpent first. There will be no forgiveness here—not for the serpent who turned the first humans against God.

The fertility cults the serpent represents are doomed to ultimately fail. They may have their moments of ascendancy, but they will ultimately be crushed, and Yahweh alone will rule in the hearts of God's people.

Now, death becomes a curse to both the man and the woman. "You are dust and to dust you shall return" is the ultimate judgment (Gen 3:19). But for the Christian, that is no longer the curse it first appears to be. Christ's death on the cross and his glorious resurrection point triumphantly to the new reality; namely, that Christ has conquered death. Saint Paul picks up the exultant cry in 1 Cor 15:54b–55: "Death has been swallowed up in victory. Where, O death is your victory? Where, O death is your sting? But thanks to God who gives us the victory in Christ Jesus our Lord."

We acknowledge the truth about ourselves: We are not God. We are instead finite human beings who sin, cross boundaries, fail, and fall short of the glory of God and so are in serious need of redemption. But there is hope, and it comes in the form of the One who said of himself, "I am the resurrection and the life. Those who believe in me, even though they die, will live, and everyone who lives and believes in me will never die" (John 11:25–26).

Then God performs one more incredibly gracious act. As the righteous yet merciful Judge of all, he overrules himself, even though no appeal has even been filed. Now he becomes a tailor and clothes the man and the woman. These are not the flimsy fig leaf garments the humans devised but genuine leather. God makes clothes for them to cover their shame. It is a clear sign of God's forgiveness and an act of incredible grace for those who so little deserved it.

This story is not about Adam and Eve so much as it is a story about you and me. Just as God was gracious to Adam and Eve, we too can claim God's abundant grace and favor as our own. The same God who created us looks upon us in mercy as human beings whom he made and whom he loves. God sees us in our confusion and blindness, and he acts. He does not condemn us, but rather reaches out with mercy and forgiveness.

Caring for the Poor and Hungry

The terrorist attack on the World Trade Center and the Pentagon on September 11, 2001, was a terrible tragedy. The unspeakable horror tore at our hearts and filled our lives with great sorrow. What followed the attack was an enormous and unprecedented outpouring of concern across the country from every segment of American life for the many who lost loved ones in the attacks.

If that same energy and concern could be harnessed on behalf of the hungry in the world, it would make a substantial difference in their lives. Addressing world hunger would not only fulfill the will of the Creator, it would bring some stability to our world, particularly in those places where hunger and injustice are the fertile soil from which terrorism takes root and sprouts and grows into deadly acts of desperation.

Although the pain and suffering caused by the World Trade Center attacks is not to be minimized, we can breathe a sigh of relief that the terrorists did not choose to target the Indian Point Nuclear Facility thirty-five miles north of Times Square. The health and environmental consequences of such a nuclear attack would have impacted the lives of future generations for longer than we can even imagine. In fact, the *9/11 Commission Report* documented that Mohammed Atta wanted to attack Indian Point, but did not get permission. Khaled Sheikh Mohammed confirmed that attacks on two nuclear facilities were in the terrorists' original plan until the attack was scaled back from ten hijacked planes to four.[6]

We whose faith is centered in the One who created resources for all to share must make every effort on behalf of the poor and hungry. What holds us back? Could it be that our riches blind us to our neighbors' need? Jesus once spoke the following words to a young man who was well versed in the law: "There is still one thing that you lack. Sell all that you have and distribute the money to the poor, and you will have treasure in heaven." (Luke 18:23).

The Genesis stories say that God meant more for us. We are meant for love, for relationship, and for community.

One way we exercise our calling to serve the Creator is through our daily work. As we saw in Gen 2:15, God established work to keep his creation going. Through us, God raises crops, hauls food to market, organizes industry, sells products, teaches the young, and keeps homes clean and safe.

God works through engineers and scientists, doctors and nurses, pastors and plumbers, farmers and secretaries, home-makers and teachers. Each of us is called to serve the Creator in our own way, with each of us using our own gifts in the setting where God has placed us. Faith is not for spectators—faith calls for people of grit and substance who are willing to roll up their sleeves and go to work for God.

6. National Commission on Terrorist Attacks, "9/11 Commission Report," 154.

3

Dark Days for the People of God

Choose life so that you and your descendants may live, loving the Lord
your God, obeying him, and holding fast to him.

Deut 30:18-20

Picture this scene: Your country lies in utter ruins. As far as
eyes can see, there is nothing but devastation. The once-fertile
fields you roamed long ago are now burnt over. This is how the
world appears after a nuclear reactor meltdown much like Fukushima Daiichi's.

This is also a picture of the world as it appeared to the Jews in
586 BCE. The temple was destroyed. Jerusalem had fallen into the
hands of the Babylonian Empire, and the Davidic line was severed.

In 586 BCE, the forces of Babylon completed their conquest
of Judah with the utter destruction of Jerusalem. Those who survived were rounded up and carried off into exile in that heathen
nation.

It is to these people in exile that the prophet speaks the divine word: "Comfort" (Isa 40:1). Notice that he does not proclaim the word once, but twice to get his point across and make sure the people hear him correctly: "God has spoken. God will act. Your struggles are over. Your sin is forgiven. All that you have suffered will soon be just a fading memory in the mist of time. So, pack up, before you know it, it will be time to go home."[1]

God's people had suffered a terrible defeat. To lose one's land is a terrible blow to any nation. It was especially horrifying to God's people, who derived their sense of identity from the land.

They knew who they were: people of God. After all, God had not forgotten them. Had God not promised the land to Abraham and Sarah? In this darkest hour, there arose from the people a hope that God would restore them to their land by acting decisively on their behalf, as God had so often done in the past. All depended on the faithfulness of the people and their trust in God. It was to this group of exiles that we owe such gems as the great creation hymn in the first chapter of Genesis and the prophetic tradition.

Isaiah retells the creation story to his people in exile, helping them keep their memories of Jerusalem—and their faith itself—alive against enormous odds in alien surroundings.

In the first story, God speaks, and things happen. Whole worlds come into existence. Gone in the J account is the great creation hymn's poetic structure. Yet both versions address the purpose and meaning of life. They displayed great creativity and courage in face of enormous suffering. What had led the people to sink to this place in its history? The answer lies in an interesting and involved history.

All three of the great monotheistic religions—Judaism, Islam, and Christianity—trace their origins to one man named Abraham. It was in response to God's call to leave behind his family and possessions in Haran and go to a land God would show him: "By faith Abraham obeyed when he was called to set out for a place that he was to receive as an inheritance, and he set out not knowing where he was going" (Heb 8:11).

1. Gugel, *Messiah*, 3.

Famine drove Jacob and his large, extended family (Abraham's decedents) to Egypt. Joseph drew on a talent for interpreting dreams to the pinnacle of power in the court of Pharaoh. Joseph had been a pariah to his brothers but was reconciled to them, and their families were invited to stay in Egypt. Their descendants became an ever-larger percentage of Egypt's population. To handle their growth, the Israelites, as they were now called, were cast into slavery. In the bitterness of their situation, the Israelites cried out to God, who heard their cry and raised up from their midst a leader named Moses. He led the Israelites to freedom through the Sea of Reeds and across the Sinai wilderness.

Much of the imagery from Exodus was incorporated into the civil rights movement of the 1960s. For example, in one of Dr. Martin Luther King's most famous sermons, he announced, "I have been to the mountain top. I have seen the promised land."[2] Compare that with the story in Deut 34:1–8, which describes God as showing Moses all of the promised land.

Under Joshua's leadership, Israel invaded the land and took control of it away from its inhabitants. But as time passed, the people were repeatedly unfaithful. Even worse, they adopted the gods of their neighbors and mixed those worship practices into their worship of the true God. God tolerated their infidelity for a time, but God's patience wore thin. It was at that point that God allowed the Israelites' neighbors to conquer them.

Roughly five hundred years go by before we encounter David. Plucked from the ranks of shepherds, he is remembered as Israel's greatest king.

Ultimately, the people cried to God for help, and God responded by sending a charismatic leader or "judge" (Samson, Gideon, and Deborah, with their different styles of leadership, are all examples) to lead them into battle to recapture the promised land. Once again, God was proven to be faithful. Finally, the people asked for a king. They saw that their neighbors had royal families and were ruled by a king, and they wanted one too. There is an old saying, "Be careful what you pray for. You just might get it."

2. See King, "I've Been to the Mountaintop."

Their first king was Saul. He began virtuously, but he grew increasingly jealous of the young shepherd-warrior David and angrily threatened David's life. David, upon Saul's death, was anointed king and under his leadership, he made Jerusalem his capital. God prevented him from building a temple. That task was left to the remarkable Solomon. No expense was spared. The building was a grandly lavish gem of a structure.

But to pay for the building, a heavy tax was levied on the people, resulting in civil war. The nation split into a northern and a southern kingdom, with Israel to the north and Judah to the south. Their rulers were uniformly wicked. (Do the names Ahab and Jezebel ring any bells?)

The north fell first to Assyria in 725 BCE, then the south in 586 BCE. The conquered nations' best and the brightest were taken into exile five hundred miles away, across some of the harshest desert known to humankind. The people needed to make a major decision: They could try to get along with their captors, á la "when in Rome, do as the Romans do." Or they could chart a different course. They could remain faithful to the God of their ancestors. They could differentiate themselves from their captors. The people chose this other path.

It was from this highly creative, strongly motivated, and intently faithful community that the great hymn of creation emerged. The people could not point to any of their recent history as evidence of God's willingness or ability to defend them. They were trapped in a pagan land and the Davidic line was irreparably broken. As the Babylonians were quick to point out, what kind of god was that? The theologians among the exiles needed to find a different, yet reliable basis for their faith.

A Faith Like Abraham's

If we were to nominate one person who emulated Abraham's' faith, it would have to be Ronald Fountain. "Each day my wife sends me off to work, confident that I am in God's arms of wisdom and safety, and that she is in God's arms of comfort." When he reported for work on March 28, 1979, he found the reactor at Three Mile Island in dangerous mode. If a stuck valve were not opened, the water in the reactor unit would boil over, and eventually it would burst into flames. The task was to open the valve and thereby let water flow into the reactor. Fountain knew that heroic activity was necessary to release the valve, exposing him to excessive radioactivity. Fountain later gave God the credit for giving him the courage needed in that dark hour and for leading him to the right spot in the pitch black darkness of the reactor.[3]

Without the temple as the center for worship, the people began to worship together in local synagogues. This practice of weekly worship, which began with a people in exile gathering in a local community of faith, was adopted centuries later by the followers of Jesus. Christians trace our practice of weekly worship back to this faithful group of exiles in Babylon. As part of *Shabbat* worship, the great stories of faith were written down and read to the gathered assembly. One member of the synagogue—a teacher, or rabbi—would then expound on the reading.

The creation story held a particularly important role in the life and consciousness of the people. That is how Gen 1 helped give the exile community an identity that sustained them throughout the long years of captivity in Babylon. This text was an important instrument in instructing young people in the truths of their faith, surrounded as they were by the claims of the Babylonian gods.

The passage is really a hymn with seven stanzas, with each stanza representing another "day" of creative activity. The repetition from one stanza to the next is in a liturgical format.

3. Huber, "We Survived," n.p.

Belief in God as the Creator became a source of hope for future deliverance from exile. In the following passage from Second Isaiah, we hear a strong word of promise from Isaiah, a prophet of the exilic community. God will deliver his people. God will return the exiles to the land of their ancestors, where they will rebuild their cities and repopulate the countryside. The proof of that is established by the declaration that God is the Creator of all that exists.

Second Isaiah's prophecies can be found in chapters 40 through 55 of the book of Isaiah. As the prophet writes,

> Thus says Yahweh, your Redeemer, who formed you in the womb: I am Yahweh, who made all things, who alone stretched out the heavens, who by myself spread out the earth . . . who says of Jerusalem, "It shall be inhabited," and of the cities of Judah, "They shall be rebuilt, and I will raise up their ruins," . . . and who says of Jerusalem, "It shall be rebuilt," and of the temple, "Your foundation shall be laid." (Isa 44:24, 26b, 28)

From the stories and legends that had been passed down over the generations from parents to children, scholars crafted a monumental piece of literature—a breathtaking hymn of praise to the supreme maker of heaven and earth.

For now, the point is to establish the liturgical and poetic nature of this first creation story and to see how the theologians of the exile, having lost the three great pillars of faith (land, Davidic succession, and temple) moved towards a creation-centered faith.

This was the nature of the faith of the exiles. Their allegiance to God was absolute. Their sense of identity and selfhood was grounded in their relationship with God. This tenacity of faith has been a part of Judaism throughout the centuries. The faith of the Jewish people has enabled them to survive in the face of serious threats to their existence at many points in history.

For example, the delightful Broadway musical, *Fiddler on the Roof* features an ongoing conversation between the Jewish character Tevye and God. Tevye does not always understand God, and he certainly does not always agree with God, but he cannot envision a life apart from God.

In a similar vein, there is a story out of the Nazi Holocaust in which prisoners in a particular concentration camp put God on trial for the Holocaust. Different prisoners played the various roles—judge, prosecutors, defense attorneys, and jury. The court proceedings continued for many nights until the case was turned over to the jury.[4]

What do you suppose the verdict was? Guilty as charged. They found God guilty of the Holocaust. The verdict was handed down, and then the rabbi led the prisoners in their evening prayers. While the prisoners pinned the blame for the Holocaust on God, it never occurred to them to desert God. To do that would be to stop being a person.

The other distinctive practices the exilic community adopted was an emphasis on Sabbath rest and on circumcision. This tradition is grounded on the unique character of the seventh day of creation, which breaks the pattern in the first six stanzas of the great hymn of praise to the Creator.

Circumcision was a radical act of faith. The foreskin does not grow back. It clearly sets a person apart. You cannot hide it. And you bear the mark for life.

To commemorate the creative activity of their God, the Jews designated the seventh day as a day of total and complete rest. If God could rest on one day, they thought, surely his people ought to do so as well. While there was to be no work performed on the seventh day, the day was not lost. The people gathered for worship and spent time in meditation on God's purposes for their lives.

Like circumcision, the Sabbath day caused the Jews to stand out in their choice to differentiate themselves from the surrounding alien culture. If the rest of the world continues its commerce and work seven days a week, it takes a strong faith to resist and instead chose a lifestyle diametrically opposed to it.

---

4. Elie Wiesel's *Trial of God*, a play set in seventeenth-century Ukraine, is said to have been based on his experience of such a trial at Auschwitz, and the account has since been made into a film by Frank Cottrell Boyce.

To stand against the rest of the world by challenging the cherished beliefs and societal practices of those in power is to risk provoking their displeasure and wrath. And yet, this hardy band of dissidents did precisely that. On a daily basis they risked the retribution of those whose authority they defied.

Those who have suffered for taking stands on issues of justice and peace know this all too well. The notion of civil disobedience is nothing new—it took place centuries ago in the great and mighty city of Babylon. Against all odds, God's people in exile held the line for God, who called forth this world by the might of God's voice.

There is always some danger in following God completely, though some times and places pose more danger than others. It is said that the seedbed of the church is watered with the blood of her martyrs and that we are never stronger in our faith than when it is put to the test. But that is to be expected. Jesus prayed for us in his high priestly prayer:

> Father, I have given them your word, and the world has hated them because they do not belong to the world, just as I do not belong to the world. I am not asking you to take them out of the world, but I ask you to protect them from the evil one. They do not belong to the world, just as I do not belong to the world. Sanctify them in the truth; your word is truth. (John 17:13–20)

This was true for the faithful men, women, and children in exile in Babylon. They recognized that they did not belong to the alien culture around them. God enabled them to survive and even flourish. The exile lasted about fifty years, ending in 539 BCE, when the exiles were permitted to return to Judah to begin rebuilding their ruined country.[5] We are the recipients of the great product of their faith: the majestic creation hymn in the opening verses of the Hebrew Scriptures.

---

5. Borg, *Reading the Bible Again*, 112.

4

Jesus Came Proclaiming the Kingdom of God

Matthew 25:31–46 is perhaps the passage in which Jesus is the clearest about what it means to live as the people of God. Justice, kindness, humility, mercy, compassion—they are all part of what it means to be human. To ignore the poor, the oppressed, the hungry, is to ignore God.

—The Green Bible[1]

Jesus came into the world at a time when the Jewish people were longing for divine intervention. They hoped for a leader, or Messiah, who would restore justice and peace to their homeland.[2] God changed the course of history through the death and resurrection of Jesus and through his disciples' mission to the world.[3]

---

1. *Green Bible*, 1230.
2. Crossan, *Jesus*, 35.
3. Spong, *Rescuing the Bible*, 123.

For Saint Paul, the resurrection of Jesus following his crucifixion was "God's yes to Jesus and God's no to the domination system."[4] The meaning of God for Saint Paul was established in Jesus' life; Jesus was the fullness of God.[5]

During Jesus' life on Earth, he built an inclusive community in which even the outcasts of society were touched by his love and grace. For Jesus, compassion was the central quality of God, and the central moral quality of life centered in God.[6]

Jesus' life revealed God's love for all of humanity. John Shelby Spong beautifully describes this all-encompassing love:

> It is that each of us, no matter how dark our shadows, or how condemned we are made to feel, are nonetheless the objects of the infinite and graceful love of God. Each of us is called to live in the wholeness of that love as one who has been embraced by the giver of infinite value. Accepting that divine valuation, we are to find the courage to be the self God has created us to be, the self we are inside the graceful gift of the righteousness of Christ.[7]

The depth of Jesus' love was beyond human understanding. As Spong further elaborates:

> It is the portrait of a life that is in touch with a reality so powerful that it has escaped all human limits. It is a picture of life so deeply loved that it has expanded to the point where it presses against every human limitation. It is this life, said the experience of the first Christians, that tested the human barrier of finitude and broke it open. Death could not and cannot contain the divine life-giving love. That was the reality behind the resurrection narratives.[8]

---

4. Borg, *Reading the Bible Again*, 125.
5. Spong, *Rescuing the Bible*, 125.
6. Ibid., 126.
7. Ibid., 238.
8. Ibid., 240.

What kind of person was Jesus? Marcus J. Borg describes the historical Jesus as a "Spirit Person," a "Social Prophet," and a "Movement Founder":

- *As a Spirit Person*, Jesus was one of those figures in human history with an experiential awareness of the reality of God. They become conduits for the power or wisdom of God to enter into this world. They experience a nonmaterial level of reality, charged with energy and power. The worldview of spirit persons is multidimensional, whereas the modern worldview is one-dimensional.

- *As a Social Prophet*, Jesus was similar to the classical prophets of ancient Israel. As such, he criticized the elites (economic, political, and religious) of his time, was an advocate of an alternative social vision, and was often in conflict with authorities.

- *As a Movement Founder*, Jesus brought into being a Jewish renewal or revitalization movement that challenged and shattered the social boundaries of his day, a movement that eventually became the early Christian Church.[9]

The coming of Jesus shifted the experience of God from knowing and belief in God to being in relationship with God. The early Christians continued to experience Jesus as a living reality after his death. The gospels contain both the early Christians' memories of Jesus of Nazareth and their ongoing experience of the resurrected Christ.[10]

Jesus came to reconcile the people to God. He is our "connection point" to God. Jesus suffered and died forgiving the people who crucified him. Jesus was God incarnate, so his forgiveness extends to all people.[11]

As Spong writes, "the Spirit of Christ within us nudges us to be more generous than we would be on our own. Awareness of

9. Borg, *Meeting Jesus Again*, 20.

10. Ibid., 31.

11. Ibid., 33.

God's forgiveness allows us to reflect God's goodness in our own halting ways, and God uses even modest acts of faith and compassion to make big changes in the world."[12]

What, then, is our hope for the world as Jesus promised and the prophets foretold? One vision offered by Hans Küng is presented below.

What Is the Kingdom of God?

It will be a kingdom where, in accordance with Jesus' prayer, God's name is truly hallowed, God's will is done on earth, [humankind] will have everything in abundance, all sin will be forgiven, and all evil will be overcome.

It will be a kingdom where, in accordance with Jesus' promises, the poor, the hungry, those who weep and those who are downtrodden will finally come into their own; where pain, suffering and death will have an end.

It will be a kingdom that cannot be described, but only made known in metaphors: as the new covenant, the seed springing up, the ripe harvest, the great banquet, the royal feast.

It will therefore be a kingdom—wholly as the prophets foretold—of absolute righteousness, of unsurpassable freedom, of dauntless love, of universal reconciliation, of everlasting peace. In this sense therefore it will be the time of salvation, of fulfillment, of consummation, of God's presence: the absolute future.[13]

—Hans Küng

---

12. Spong, *Rescuing the Bible*, 123.

13. Küng, *On Being a Christian*, 215.

5

Justice According to God

It is possible to have a new kind of world, a world where there will be more compassion, more gentleness, more caring, more laughter, for this is God's dream.[1]

—Archbishop Desmond Tutu

The following statement appeared as a true/false question on a test I administered to my class of seventh graders in our parish confirmation program: "In God's eyes, justice means upholding the powerless and holding the powerful accountable." This was a setup for a "teachable moment" since I suspected that most students would get it wrong. The correct answer is true.

I knew that it would give my students one more opportunity to learn this central Biblical teaching—that God's justice is grounded in God's upholding the powerless and holding the

1. Qtd. in *Green Bible*, I–14.

powerful accountable. The students felt the meaning of the word "justice" was limited to the following definitions:

1. Fair Play

2. Lawfulness

3. Due punishment deserved

4. The US system, including courts at various levels

God intends all the resources on the earth to be shared rather than hoarded or wasted by a privileged few. President Dwight D. Eisenhower, in the waning days of his second term in office, made the following observation about the arms race, "Every gun that is made, every warship launched, every rocket fired, signifies in the final sense a theft from those who hunger and are not fed, those who are cold and are not clothed."[2]

God's justice calls for sharing resources, not hoarding them, and certainly not wasting them. God has ensured that there is plenty for all to share. God condemns all who exploit the poor. Everyone will be judged according to what they have done or failed to do. The criteria are: Did they respond to the poor? Did they see Jesus in the poor and respond accordingly? When they saw Jesus in the hungry person before them, did they feed him? When they saw him thirsty, did they give him something to drink?

Efforts to feed hungry people, for example, were not on the radar screens of my seventh graders. God's justice demands that we oppose any effort to rob from the poor and hungry. It requires that we lift them up, giving them first place in our thinking and in our political life. Yet the needs of the poor are deliberately overlooked when utility companies begin to build these nuclear monsters.

"To do justice is to correct the systems that unfairly harm the poor."[3] Obviously, to hand out Thanksgiving or Christmas food baskets while not addressing the issues of *why* people are hungry is to condemn the poor in their distress.

---

2. Dwight David Eisenhower, "The Chance for Peace," speech given to the American Society of Newspaper Editors, April 16, 1953.

3. Aeschliman, "Loving the Earth," I–94.

This problem manifests itself when too few have too much and too many have too little. Hunger robs people of their health, saps their strength, and hastens their early death.

Nuclear energy literally robs. First it concentrates capital in one place when that money could be used in so many more productive, helpful, and less risky ways; and secondly, it forces a captive group that is given little choice (the customer base) when it comes time to pay up. This represents stealing by the rich from the pockets of the poor. Poverty robs so many people of the opportunity to live full and productive lives. We must persevere until every child of God has enough food to eat, decent shelter, and a hopeful future for themselves and their families.

For God to exercise preference toward the poor is more than the picture of a referee who plays favorites. It has everything to do with our role in life, our calling, and our destiny as the people of God. It is a clear call to action: *We must not be condemned to live with nuclear power forever.*

Walter Brueggemann identifies the "myth of scarcity."[4] Brueggemann's use of this term suggests that when we begin to acquire stuff, there are never enough resources to protect us against every eventuality.[5]

An opportunity for reflection on what had landed God's people in exile came in the form of a word of judgment and a word of hope for the not-too-distant future: if they could remain faithful, God would soon deliver the means to restore them to their land. Various prophets came on the scene. Among them were Amos, Micah, Hosea, and Isaiah.

How are we doing? Here are some statistics on world hunger:

4. Brueggemann, "Liturgy of Abundance," 2.

5. Keynote address at Bread for the World National Conference. See Stephenson, "We Are Takers," http://blog.bread.org/2011/11/we-are-takers-a-prayer-by-walter-brueggemann.html.

World Hunger by the Numbers

- 800 million people are malnourished (one-sixth of the world's population).
- 24,000 people die each day from hunger or hunger-related illnesses (three-fourths are children).
- 10 percent of children die before age five.
- 880 million people lack access to adequate health care.
- 1:420 is the doctor to patient ratio in the developed world.
- 1:7,000 is the doctor to patient ratio in the developing world.
- 1:30,000 is the doctor to patient ratio in sub-Saharan Africa.
- 1.3 billion people lack access to safe drinking water.
- 57 is the life expectancy in developing nations (it is even lower for women).
- 80 percent of HIV-positive patients live in the developing world.
- Food accounts for 16.4 percent of spending for households making less than $10,000 per year compared to the US average of 12.7 percent.[6]

Those are staggering statistics. When a Boeing 777 jumbo jet was shot down by a missile over Ukraine with eighty children aboard, it made headlines the world over. And yet millions of children die each year from hunger-related diseases and we hear nothing. If we are to deal with world hunger and bring it to an end, we need to face this brutal information head-on.

The prophets' message was clear and went to the heart of the problem. The prophets proclaimed the truth that God took the side of the poor. God needed to step in on behalf of the poor and

6. Bread for the World Institute, "About Hunger," http://www.bread.org/who-experiences-hunger.

powerless since no one else would. The Hebrew Scriptures in particular link God's creation of the world to God's executing justice.[7] How long this goes on is up to us. The fact that people will suffer as a result of nuclear power should wake us up. It depends neither on a nuclear disaster nor the scheduled release of radioactive substances into the atmosphere. Nuclear power is dangerous from start to finish.

The following verse from the Psalms sums up this entire chapter on God's justice: "I know that the Lord maintains the cause of the needy and executes justice for the poor" (Ps 140:12).

The promotion of nuclear power plants is itself a criminal act of great proportions since nuclear power plants are granted licenses—licenses to kill. Indeed, "Nuclear power is a violation of human rights and justice."[8]

"Many of the undernourished children who survive infancy never realize their physical or intellectual potential. Hunger hurts adults, too. Undernourished adults lack energy and are less productive than they could be."[9]

Micah's prophetic words pull listeners back to the covenant God made with the nation of Israel. But there's twist in his message: God's part of the covenant is mercy and care and redemption. The human part is to live as people of justice, kindness, and humility.[10]

When the Bible uses the term "justice" it means something totally different than how we use it on a day-to-day basis. The Hebrew Scriptures in particular link God's creation of the world to God's executing justice, as is seen in Ps 146 beginning at verse 5. Creation and justice are two sides of the same coin—they are inseparable.

> Happy are those whose help is the God of Jacob, whose hope is in Yahweh their God, who made heaven and earth, the sea, and all that is in them; who keeps faith

7. Borg, *Reading the Bible Again*, 138.

8. Reader, *Atom's Eve*, 224.

9. Beckmann, *Exodus from Hunger*, 21.

10. *Green Bible*, 1229.

forever; who executes justice for the oppressed; who gives food to the hungry. Yahweh sets the prisoners free; Yahweh opens the eyes of the blind. Yahweh lifts up those who are bowed down; Yahweh loves the righteous. Yahweh watches over the strangers; he upholds the orphan and the widow, but the way of the wicked he brings to ruin. (Ps 146: 5–9)

Many of the prophets of the Hebrew Scriptures severely criticized Israel when the people and their leaders sought to practice injustice, as in Amos:

Because you trample on the poor and take from them levies of grain, you have built houses of hewn stone, but you shall not live in them; you have planted pleasant vineyards, but you shall not drink their wine. For I know how many are your transgressions, and how great are your sins—you who afflict the righteous, who take a bribe, and push aside the needy in the gate. Seek good and not evil, that you may live; and so Yahweh, the god of hosts, will be with you. Hate evil and love good, and establish justice in the gate; it may be that Yahweh, the God of hosts, will be gracious to the remnant of Joseph. (Amos 5:11–13)

Nowhere is God's own unique justice celebrated with greater clarity and joy than in Mary's Magnificat:

My soul magnifies the Lord and my spirit rejoices in God my Savior. His mercy is for those who fear him from generation to generation. He has shown strength with his arm; he has scattered the proud in the thoughts of their hearts. He has brought down the powerful from their thrones, and lifted up the lowly; he has filled the hungry with good things, and sent the rich away empty. (Luke 1: 50–53)

It is clear that we as a human race have heavy work to do and serious choices to make if we are to pass on a livable world to our children and to all the children of the world.

Having dominion over the whole of creation means that we have a responsibility to help those burdened with poverty. We have a responsibility to be productive, to share and not waste precious God-given resources, to feed the hungry, and to seek justice for those oppressed by the powerful.

In their seminal work, *Resident Aliens: Life in the Christian Colony* Stanley Hauerwas and William Willimon describe what it means to be a people living in exile surrounded by an increasingly alien culture sinking into a morass of individualism and materialism. Their analysis brings to mind the exilic community in Babylon. Those people struggled mightily to remain faithful to Yahweh, the God of their ancestors.

We begin our lives "in paradise," but we all experience expulsion into a world of exile, anxiety, self-preoccupation, bondage, and conflict. And yes, this is also a world of goodness and beauty—it is God's creation. But it is a world in which something is awry. The rest of the Bible is largely made up of stories about this state of affairs: the human predicament and its solution.

In his inaugural address, Amos indicts the wealthy for their exploitation of the poor: "You oppress the poor and crush the needy. You trample on the poor and take from them taxes of grain. You trample on the needy, and bring to ruin the poor of the land" (Amos 5:11). What, then, does God want? Amos continues, "But let justice roll down like waters, and righteousness like an ever-flowing stream" (Amos 5:24).[11]

Outrage against nuclear power has decreased, according to a recent poll that found 71 percent of those surveyed supported nuclear power.[12] But the National Council of Churches has declared a policy statement on energy[13] whose principles can be summarized as follows:

- Christians must be guided by values based on the biblical witness to creation, redemption, stewardship, justice, and hope. These values should shape the policy decisions necessary to

11. Borg, *Reading the Bible Again*, 118–19.

12. Grunwald, "Real Cost," 2.

13. Reader, Atom's Eve, 241.

meet the profound challenge facing humanity: how to share limited amounts of energy fairly without poisoning ourselves by poisoning the wider environment.

- Persons are unique in their capacity to respond to God in faith and hope, to their human neighbors with love, and to the nonhuman part of creation with respect and responsible care.

- When faith in the Creator and in the Kingdom of God is replaced by faith in human ability to solve all problems by technical means, humanity has also fallen into the sin of idolatry.

- If using a technology poses a risk of irreversible global damage, great prudence and caution should be exercised in deciding about its use. The greater the risk, the less moral justification there is for its use.

- We have committed crimes against humanity through our gross negligence and irresponsibility.

In contrast to these principles, the Fukushima Daiichi meltdowns demonstrated the fallibility of Japan's faith in our technological abilities. The writer Haruki Murakami spoke of such hubris pointedly:

> This is a historic experience for us Japanese: our second massive nuclear disaster. But this time no one dropped a bomb on us. We set the stage, we committed the crime with our own hands, we are destroying our own lands, and we are destroying our own lives. While we are the victims, we are also the perpetrators. We must fix our eyes on this fact. If we fail to do so, we will inevitably repeat the same mistake again, somewhere else.[14]

Germany has resolved to phase out nuclear power by 2022. Austria, Italy, and Switzerland have also reconsidered its use.[15]

In the United States, the Nuclear Regulatory Commission found no "imminent threat" from an inspection of US nuclear

14. Haruki Murakami, qtd. in Osnos, "Fallout," 10.

15. Hockenos, "Nuclear Power," 1.

reactors.[16] This was despite its conclusion that about a third of the reactors had some emergency equipment that might be vulnerable to extreme circumstances, such as fires and explosions, in ways that are startlingly reminiscent of the conditions at Fukushima Daiichi. At one plant, a single, diesel-driven pump was incapable of providing emergency water to both of the on-site reactors. At another plant, firefighting equipment was stored in a building not fortified to withstand an earthquake because a severe fire and an earthquake "were not assumed to occur coincidentally," according to the report.[17]

A Japanese widow who decided to stay on her farm near Fukushima stated, "It wasn't just the Tokyo Electric Power Company that caused all this. It was all of us who lived and enjoyed the benefits."[18] Indeed, as US Senator Elizabeth Warren warns, "There is nobody in this country who got rich on his own. Nobody. You built a factory out there? Good for you. But I want to be clear: You moved your goods to market on the roads the rest of us paid for; you hired workers the rest of us paid to educate; you were safe in your factory because of police forces and fire forces that the rest of us paid for."[19]

As individuals, we may not be directly responsible for the exploitative power structure that lies behind nuclear energy, enriching the few while endangering the many, but we can all take responsibility for helping to change it. As activists, we can work to end hunger and poverty by advocating for cleaner, more equitable energy. It may not be easy to build an energy system that treats people and the world we live in according to our Christian conscious, but it can be done, for as Dr. Martin Luther King Jr. said, "Every step toward the goal of justice requires sacrifice, suffering,

---

16. Osnos, "Fallout," 11.

17. Ibid.

18. Ibid.

19. Senator Warren made these statements in Andover, Massachusetts, during her talking tour in September of 2011. Elizabeth Warren, qtd. in Benen, "Underlying Social Contract," http://www.washingtonmonthly.com/political-animal/2011_09/the_underlying_social_contract032342.php.

and struggle."[20] Dr. King further said, "If you are cut down in a movement that is designed to save the soul of a nation, then no other death could be more redemptive . . . We must somehow believe that unearned suffering is redemptive . . . We must work passionately and indefatigably to bridge the gulf between our scientific progress and our moral progress. One of the great problems of mankind is that we suffer from a poverty of the spirit which stands in glaring contrast to our scientific and technological abundance. The richer we have become materially, the poorer we have become morally and spiritually."[21]

In his book *Exodus from Hunger*, Bread for the World president David Beckmann reminds that God's presence in the movement to overcome hunger and poverty raises our hopes. Real accomplishments in recent decades are also cause for optimism. Beckmann emphasizes that doing our part to overcome hunger and poverty is crucial to religious integrity: "We can go to church and sing great hymns, but if we don't help people in need, this is made-up religion rather than connection to the real God. We can read spiritual books and pursue a wholesome lifestyle, but if we don't help people in need, our faith remains self-centered."[22]

Pope Francis has given an example of identifying with the poor and hungry of the world:

In 1998 Pope John Paul II and Archbishop Desmond Tutu both suggested that the millennium year, 2000, be celebrated by canceling the debts of poor countries. They referred to the book of Leviticus in the Bible, which called for a jubilee every fifty years. In that jubilee year, all debts would be forgiven and the land returned to its original owners. The idea had power, and British activists began to organize the international Jubilee campaign.[23]

In the Jubilee campaign, I was a part of a large crowd of activists gathered on the mall in Washington, DC. After an afternoon of speech-making, we headed to the capitol and held hands,

20. Martin Luther King Jr., qtd. in Beckmann, *Exodus from Hunger*, 76.

21. King and King, *Words of Martin Luther King*, 67.

22. Ibid., 77.

23. Ibid., 95.

symbolically forming a human chain around the entire building. It was quite dramatic, as we were asking Congress to break the chains of debt that held so many nations back. The eventual solution: "debt reduction for countries with credible poverty reduction strategies" was passed by Congress and signed into law by President Clinton.[24]

The results were impressive. The Jubilee Campaign of 1999–2000 started a process that has reduced the debt obligations of thirty relatively well-governed poor countries by $78 billion. Those nations are paying $3 billion less in debt service every year, which has allowed for an increase in annual funding for basic health and education.[25] Debt relief was the key.

In order to extend the life of America's remaining ninety-nine nuclear reactors, the US Nuclear Regulatory Commission voted to lower safety standards on many of those reactors. This is a call to action to confront the actual number-one crisis facing America today: the reckless endangerment of the people of this nation through the risky presence of nuclear power.

24. Ibid.
25. Ibid., 99.

6

Health Risks

I see skies of blue and clouds of white.
The bright blessed day, the dark sacred night.
And I think to myself, what a wonderful world.

—Louis Armstrong[1]

Would you allow your child to play in the park if there was a poisonous snake loose somewhere within it, however tiny the probability of being bitten? What if the snake was invisible and its bite caused cancer or leukemia? What then?

Weighing the risks of exposure to harm is never easy. How are we, as parents, citizens, public health advocates, nuclear workers, and policy makers, to judge what is an acceptable risk, especially when the exposure is difficult to measure and the health effects present themselves years later?

---

1. Qtd. in *Green Bible*, I–112.

Health Risks

The health risks posed by nuclear power production are serious and long lasting. Exposure to nuclear radiation is harmful in chronic, low-level doses as well as acute, high-level doses. Both levels of exposure can carry over into future generations. It is nearly impossible to eliminate all risk of exposure from nuclear power because the radioactive isotopes essentially live on forever.

In 1977, the US Nuclear Regulatory Commission published a diagram (see below) illustrating the many pathways humans can be exposed to routine radioactive releases from nuclear power plants.[2] A close look at the diagram reveals how our air, water, and soil becomes contaminated and how radioactive particles enter our bodies through the air we breathe, the water we drink, and the food we eat. These radioactive particles can also be absorbed through our skin.

Helen Caldicott, a physician and the world's leading spokesperson about the dangers of nuclear power, explained the health risks in her 2006 book, *Nuclear Power Is Not the Answer*. Dr. Caldicott described the incidence of cancer among nuclear reactor workers and their children, uranium miners, indigenous peoples living near nuclear waste sites, and everyday people exposed through contaminated soil used in urban development projects. This is what she found:

- One in five nuclear workers is predicted to develop cancer after receiving the "legally allowable" dose over many years of exposure.[3]

- Children born to parents who have been exposed to radiation have a higher-than-normal risk of developing cancer or leukemia.[4]

- One-fifth to one-half of uranium miners have died of lung cancer in North America, many of whom were Native Americans. The same is true in Germany, Namibia, and Russia.[5]

2. Beyond Nuclear, "Routine Radioactive Releases," 1.
3. Caldicott, *Nuclear Power*, 45.
4. Ibid.
5. Ibid., 48.

ROUTINE RADIOACTIVE RELEASES FROM U.S. NUCLEAR POWER PLANTS

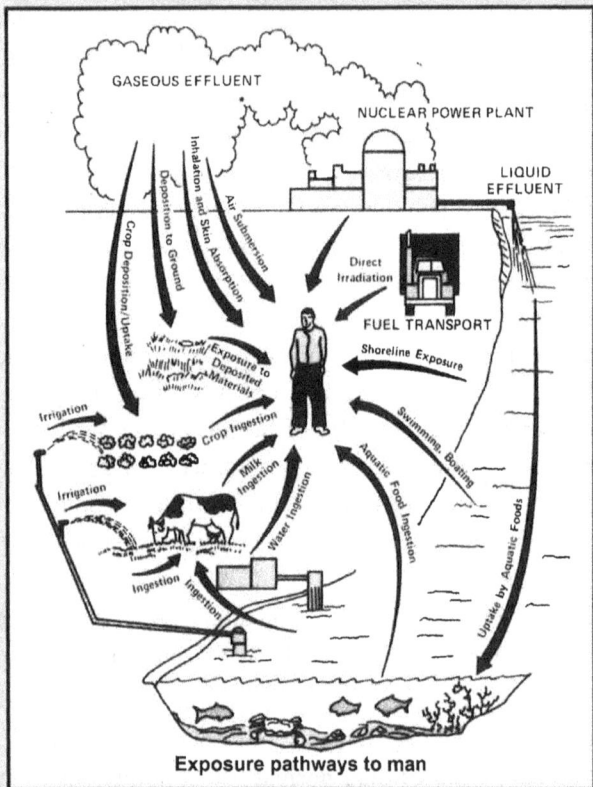

Exposure pathways to man

↑A DIAGRAM PUBLISHED IN 1977 BY THE U.S. NUCLEAR REGULATORY COMMISSION

Caldicott explains how exposure to radiation in the environment causes cancer in the human body. In the mines, exposure to high concentrations of the radioactive gas that accumulates in mines' air supply (which, if inhaled, can decay in the lungs and form deposits in the respiratory passages) can irradiate cells that then become malignant. Additionally, when miners swallow uranium dust, radium is absorbed through the gut and forms deposits in their bones. Uranium itself also accumulates in bone, and it too is carcinogenic.[6]

These dangerous chemicals have also inadvertently harmed workers outside the nuclear industry. Caldicott shares the story of female workers who, in the early part of the twentieth century, painted numbers on watch dials with radium enriched paint that made the numbers glow in the dark. To make the figures precise, they licked the tips of their paintbrushes, thereby swallowing large amounts of radium. Because radium is a calcium analogue, it deposited in their bones. Many of these women subsequently died of osteogenic sarcoma, a highly malignant bone cancer affecting their facial bones, while others succumbed to leukemia, a disease affecting the white blood cells manufactured in bone marrow.[7]

Besides the workers, the general public is exposed to radiation from the waste that is discarded and left lying in huge heaps adjacent to the mine, exposed to the air and the rain.[8] This radioactive dirt, called mill tailings, constantly leaks radon 220 and thorium—a dangerous element with a half-life of 80,000 years—into the air, causing lung cancer. Over the last forty years, over 100 million tons of mill tailings have accumulated in the American Southwest, much of it on indigenous tribal lands in the Four Corners area at the intersection of Arizona, Colorado, New Mexico, and Utah. "By 1980, the sovereign Navajo nation had forty-two uranium mines and seven mills located on or adjacent to reservation or trust land."[9]

Groundwater has been contaminated from the byproducts of the nuclear weapons production. If uranium 235 is enriched above a concentration of 50 percent, it can be used as nuclear weapons fuel.[10] While workers can be exposed during the enrichment

6. Ibid., 49.
7. Ibid.
8. Ibid.
9. Ibid., 49–50. See also ibid., 62–63.
10. Ibid., 51.

process, it is the discarded material, uranium 238, that is most dangerous. Thousands of leaking, disintegrating barrels of this nuclear waste are sitting at enrichment facilities such as Paducah, Kentucky, awaiting disposal. Meanwhile, the government has been forced to provide alternative drinking water for local residents.[11]

We have entered into the use of nuclear power without understanding the seriousness of the health risks. A prime example is what happened in Grand Junction, Colorado, in the mid–1960s, as told by Caldicott:

> Local contractors there discovered acres of discarded mill tailings, unguarded and untreated. Not knowing they were radioactive, the contractors used them for cheap landfill and in concrete mix. Schools, hospitals, private homes, roads, an airport, and a shopping mall were constructed using this material. In 1970, local pediatricians noticed an increased incidence of cleft lip, cleft palate, and other congenital anomalies among newborn babies born to parents who lived in these radioactive structures, which continually emitted gamma radiation and radon gas.[12]

The Environmental Protection Agency initiated a study of the incident, but it was not completed due to budget cuts.

Another example of the harm caused from underestimating the health risks of nuclear power is what happened on Long Island in the 1970s and 1980s. As Caldicott explains,

> An old, dirty reactor at Brookhaven National Labs released large amounts of radiation for many years, and an epidemic of a very rare form of cancer called rhabdomyosarcoma appeared in children living near that reactor. This highly malignant muscle cancer could be caused by exposure to cesium 137, one of 200 isotopes contained in nuclear waste.[13]

11. Ibid., 51–52.
12. Ibid.
13. Ibid., 64.

Health Risks

Acute radiation sickness is caused when people are exposed to high-level, whole-body doses of radiation, such as the levels of exposure caused by catastrophic nuclear accidents like Three Mile Island in the United States and Chernobyl in Ukraine. Symptoms of acute radiation sickness include nausea, vomiting, diarrhea, bleeding from the nose, a metallic taste in the mouth, hair loss, and skin rashes.[14]

Surprisingly, security at nuclear power plants is far from adequate, despite the upgrades in response to the 9/11 terrorist attacks "even though these facilities constitute potential weapons of mass destruction and, as such, are inviting targets for terrorists. In truth, terrorists do not need their own weapons of mass destruction, as such weapons are conveniently deployed all over the world next to large and strategically important populations."[15]

Even more alarming considering the nuclear disaster in Japan, recently revised emergency planning protocols (developed by nuclear power regulators) now require fewer exercises for major accidents and recommend that fewer people be evacuated right away. In addition, the mandate that local responders always run practice exercises for a radiation release has been eliminated. When nuclear power plants shut down, emergency preparedness is still necessary due to the risks posed by high-level radioactive waste, and yet the NRC will permit ending such procedures.[16]

Chris Busby is a physical chemist, an independent researcher on the effects of low-level radiation, and the author of *Wings of Death: Nuclear Pollution and Human Health*. Busby argues that pollution caused by nuclear weapons production and nuclear power generation presents serious environmental and human health risks. For example, he claims that the incidence of childhood leukemia is several times higher than average in areas surrounding nuclear facilities. Busby asserts that radioactive fission

14. Ibid.

15. Ibid., 89.

16. See Beyond Nuclear, "NRC Denies," http://www.beyondnuclear.org/nuclear-power/2014/4/9/nrc-denies-modest-post-fukushima-emergency-response-recommen.html.

products cause genetic damage that leads to all types of cancer and other illnesses such as heart disease.

So *would* you allow your child to play in the park with a poisonous snake loose?

The hidden harm caused by nuclear power plants was summarized this way by John Gofman, who serves as Professor Emeritus of Medical Physics at the University of California Berkeley and Chairman of the Committee for Nuclear Responsibility:

> Nuclear power starts to commit murder when the plant goes into operation. It does so by guaranteeing that people are going to be poisoned for hundreds of thousands of years by radon and its daughter products brought to the surface of the earth in the course of mining the uranium needed to operate the nuclear plants. Had these substances remained in the bowels of the earth, they would have done no harm to anyone.
>
> And the random murder of citizens is further increased by the fact that there are emissions of radioactive substances both in the normal and abnormal operation of the nuclear fuel cycle. Just how large the number of people to be murdered is dependent upon the outcome of the largest experiment upon humans that evil genius has yet concocted.[17]

17. See John Gofman, "Law versus Justice," in Reader, *Atom's Eve*, 225.

7

Dollars and Nonsense

What exactly is nuclear power? It is a very expensive, sophisticated, and dangerous way to boil water.

—Helen Caldicott[1]

Imagine you are seated in the showroom at a local automobile dealership. You want to purchase a new car. The salesperson warns that the model you picked could explode at any time, especially during an earthquake or a tsunami.

Also, she can't quote you a price, only that it far exceeds what the sticker shows, and she can't arrange financing either. Do not be surprised, she tells you, to find the car will be spending a great deal of time in the shop for repairs, lengthy tune-ups, and scheduled refueling. Also, while it boasts many safety features, unfortunately the only way to test them is through an actual crash. And then it will be too late. The destruction will be overwhelming.

1. Caldicott, *Nuclear Power*, 4.

Then what about a used car, you inquire. Her face lights up: "I have just what you're looking for—a 1973 Oldsmobile!" The annual cost of fuel for this model will surprise you. There are a few dings here and there and it is rusted out in spots, but it's only forty years old.

This is what the nuclear industry is trying to sell the American people—new and used nuclear power plants. And it takes loads of money to build these behemoths. But not to worry, Congress comes to the rescue with billions of dollars in government subsidies in the form of loan guarantees, thus tying up capital that could be spent in so many other constructive and helpful ways.

Without the support of the federal government, there would be no nuclear program; it would cease to exist. Wall Street won't invest in nuclear power plants. Lines of credit have dried up for the nuclear industry. Bankers and investment brokers feel they are taking on too much risk. They would much prefer natural gas or coal-fired power plants. Nuclear power is expanding only in places where taxpayers and ratepayers can be compelled to foot the bill.

Thousands of AARP (American Association of Retired People) members in Iowa contacted lawmakers in that state in the spring of 2011 to oppose legislation that would allow utility companies to raise rates and so force consumers to bear the up-front costs of building a nuclear power plant. If construction were canceled at any point, ratepayers would have to pick up the tab not only for accrued costs, but also to assure a profit for the utility company.[2]

There are ninety-nine nuclear power plants licensed to churn out electricity in the United States. At the present time, no new nuclear power plants are on schedule to be built. However, in some places, such as in Georgia, construction has begun to add capacity to existing power plants. The Georgia project is projected to cost roughly $14 billion. If past history is any guide, that $14 billion is just the beginning of an expensive run-up in costs.

2. Carroll, "AARP Survey," http://assets.aarp.org/rgcenter/general/iowa-voters-advance-ratemaking-legislation.pdf.

At every step of the nuclear fuel chain, Congress provides subsidies and dollars from the Department of Defense's weapons development budget. The total cost of these monsters is difficult to pin down because the Defense Department buried the cost under the development of atomic weapons and because there are subsidies for uranium mining. Inevitably, massive cost overruns develop, and costs have indeed rocketed out of sight. With the federal budget as tight as it currently is, surely better uses could be found for these funds. Proponents of nuclear energy have spent billions of dollars obtaining favors from members of Congress in both parties. Conflicts of interest also occur among nuclear regulators in both Japan and the United States, whose regulators frequently find lucrative jobs in the industries they are intended to police.[3]

Once they are built, nuclear power plants are expensive to operate. If a unit fails, there are limits to the liability the owners are required to assume. Now, ask yourself this question: If the reactors were as safe as the atomic industry claims, would liability limits be necessary? The Price-Anderson Act signed by President Eisenhower and upheld by the Supreme Court protects the nuclear industry by limiting the industry's liability. The nuclear industry's share in the event of a nuclear meltdown is 2 percent. The government's share is 98 percent, topping out at $600 billion per incident.

With nuclear power, you only get one chance to get it right. Those are not favorable odds if one values human life. It has been roughly forty years since the last nuke came online. During the intervening years, it is safe to assume that the pool of available engineers and scientists has constricted. They have not been honing their skills, learning more about nuclear power generation, or working at solutions to new nuclear problems. It is not like driving a car. If you were a young person making a career choice, would nuclear engineering be at the top of your list? Not likely.

As nuclear power reactors age, their age shows in increasing technical failures. Anybody with an old house or an older automobile knows what we're talking about. Half of the aging nuclear power plants are leaking radioactive tritium through cracks in the

3. Osnos, "Fallout," 6.

reactor systems, structures, and components. Even though today's reactors were designed for a forty-year life span, the Nuclear Regulatory Commission, acceding to industry pressure, has approved twenty-year extensions to the original forty-year licenses for nuclear power plants.[4]

So, we may ask, why doesn't the Nuclear Regulatory Commission just banish nuclear power? Other nations are phasing out their nuclear programs. After the Fukushima Daiichi disaster, Chancellor Angela Merkel announced that Germany is phasing out its nuclear program. The fact that General Electric (otherwise known as Hitachi), Halliburton, Bechtel, and Toshiba (otherwise known as Westinghouse) are among the most well-connected corporations in the country may explain this conundrum.

At the dawning of the Nuclear Age, there was an expectation that one day nuclear power would be so cheap that we would not even require meters. That dream has become a nightmare. Nuclear power will never live up to its promise.

Accidents happen. Before Fukushima Daiichi blew up, there was Chernobyl. Located on the steppes of the Ukraine, it exploded, blanketing Europe under a thick radioactive cloud. Many people blamed Chernobyl on Soviet incompetence, but the same charge cannot be leveled against the Japanese, who gave the world the Toyota Prius. The Fukushima Daiichi is an American design—a General Electric Mark I boiling water reactor—built and operated by the Japanese nuclear industry.[5]

Additionally, one might think that if there ever were a country that would be extra careful handling all things nuclear, it would be Japan, the only country nuclear weapons were used against in World War II. And yet, we have the recent disaster at the Fukushima Daiichi plant. When will we face up to the fact that nuclear power is a failed technology?

In the United States, the 1979 nuclear accident at the Three Mile Island plant in Pennsylvania was triggered by a valve malfunction. Poorly trained operators working in a control room

4. Baynton, "Perils of Nuclear Power," 1.

5. Beyond Nuclear, ""Fukushima 4 Years On" 5.

of inferior design overrode the safety mechanism, causing the meltdown.[6]

It is alarming that the Indian Point nuclear reactor in New York sits astride an earthquake fault line. Indian Point is a mere thirty-five miles north of Times Square. Imagine attempting to evacuate Manhattan in the event of a nuclear explosion.

It is uncertain, even doubtful, that the amount of energy generated from a nuclear power plant is greater than the amount of energy expended during production. The US government covers the costly step of mining and milling uranium fuel, but as Helen Caldicott explains, there are high energy costs associated with each step in the nuclear fuel chain:

> The nuclear industry myth says that nuclear power costs only 1.9 cents per kilowatt hour, whereas coal costs 1.8 cents and gas-fired power costs 5.7 cents. But these figures apply only to nuclear energy generated from existing nuclear reactors. They represent a classic omission of capital costs from a pricing equation. Electricity from old nuclear reactors is relatively cheap because all the initial costs of construction, regulatory delays, and the like have been long forgotten.[7]

In fact, many citizens would be shocked to discover that:

> The United States government spent a gargantuan $111.5 billion on energy research and development between 1948 and 1998, allocating 60 percent or $70 billion of this to the nuclear industry alone. Over the same fifty years, $26 billion was allocated to oil, coal, and natural gas; $12 billion went to renewable energy sources such as wind, hydro, geothermal, and solar power; and only $8 billion went to energy efficiency technologies.[8]

---

6. Grunwald, "Real Cost," 2.

7. Caldicott, *Nuclear Power*, 19.

8. Ibid., 21.

U.S. Government Spending on Energy Research and Development
1948–1998

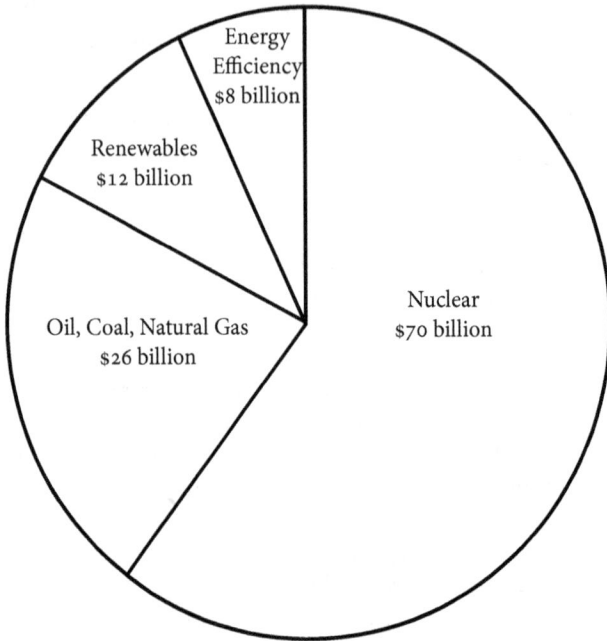

Energy
Efficiency
$8 billion

Renewables
$12 billion

Oil, Coal, Natural Gas
$26 billion

Nuclear
$70 billion

Based on this information, we can conclude that "despite the fact that most developed countries are rhetorically wedded to principles of the 'free market,' their governments remain inexplicably enthusiastic about a form of energy that cannot be sustained without huge government subsidies and handouts."[9]

So, we must ask ourselves if we would buy a car from such a dealership. Cost and safety are often top concerns when we are shopping for a new car. We know that we must be savvy shoppers to avoid being taken advantage of by the dealer. The same is true with the push for nuclear power. We must be informed citizens and question whether our limited national resources are better spent on more pressing concerns that do not place our planet and people at risk for grave harm.

9. Abraham and Tucker, *Lights Out*, 13.

8

What Are We Doing with All This Waste?

The fission reactor produces both energy and radioactive waste; we want to use the energy now and leave the radioactive waste for our children and grandchildren to take care of.

—Hannes Alfvén, 1970 Nobel laureate in physics[1]

One of the most intractable conundrums of the Nuclear Age is what to do with waste, some of which lies in piles "70-years deep."[2] The piles keep growing, and no solution appears on the horizon.

A fraction of the plutonium that is separated from reprocessing is intended for use in new reactor fuel. When used, however, the new fuel itself generates even more plutonium and other

1. Qtd. in Beyond Nuclear, "Nuclear Power and Children," 2.
2. Ibid., "Lethal Legacy," 1.

long-lived radioactive wastes. Plutonium-239 continues releasing harmful particles and rays for at least 240,000 years.[3]

No safe technology or disposal site exists to isolate the radioactive wastes that reprocessing generates. Because the solid irradiated rods are transformed into high-level radioactive liquids and sludge, reprocessing increases rather than decreases the volume of homeless radioactive waste. The waste byproducts cannot be reused. They have to be abandoned on-site or dumped elsewhere, and the environmental releases from reprocessing are large-scale.

Radioactive waste is not only dangerous now, but some remains dangerous virtually forever. Each type of radioactive isotope continues to give off rays and radioactive particles at a constant rate regardless of the temperature, pressure, or chemical environment until it decays into a different radioactive or stable isotope. Nothing can alter or stop this rate.[4]

What is worse is the fact that the extracted plutonium can be easily converted to weapons-grade material. This fact alone means we must bring an end to nuclear power. Security is wildly insufficient at most nuclear power plants. If a rogue state or a band of terrorists were to target a nuclear power plant for its radioactive waste, there would be little to stop them. Washington state officials are concerned that six underground tanks full of radioactive waste are leaking. Cleanup is expected to last decades and cost billions of dollars, according to a February 16, 2013 article.[5]

Nature can be ruthless in collaboration with radioactive waste. In the summer of 2011 a wildfire broke out in Arizona—the worst wildfire in that state's history. Before the blaze was contained, it would consume entire square miles, crossing over into New Mexico and bearing down on the city of Los Alamos, threatening the city's huge number of barrels filled with radioactive waste in "temporary" storage.

3. Ibid., "Dirty, Dangerous and Expensive," 3.

4. Ibid., 2.

5. "Tank Storing Radioactive Waste Leaking in Washington," http://www.cnn.com/2013/02/15/us/washington-tank-leak/.

Proposals have been made, but every time a proposal has been announced, the forces of NIMBY ("Not in my backyard") have gone into overdrive. Once, plans were made to bury the waste under Yucca Mountain in Nevada. Then it was discovered that the site was on a seismic fault, plus the water runoff was used for irrigation and for drinking. The project was abandoned after some $400 million had been spent on its development. But the Department of Energy has projected Yucca's price tag at around $100 billion, if it does go forward.[6]

Then there is the whole matter of shipping nuclear waste. No one wants to have radioactive waste trundling through their towns. Whether by rail, truck, or barge, accidents can and do happen, more often than we would like.

There are two levels of waste—high-level waste and low-level waste. High-level waste consists of the spent fuel rods as they come out of the reactor for refueling. Low-level waste is everything else that has accumulated since the earliest days of the Nuclear Age some seventy years ago. Some low-level waste is highly radioactive and could deliver a fatal dose of gamma radiation within twenty minutes. Several states have paved the way on this issue by imposing a moratorium on new construction until this problem is solved.

General Electric has successfully tested laser enrichment for two years and is seeking federal permission to build a $1 billion plant that would make reactor fuel by the ton. That might be good news for the nuclear industry, but critics fear that if the work succeeds, rogue states and terrorists could make bomb fuel in much smaller, difficult to detect plants. Not likely to happen here? Ask that question of the residents of Boston who experienced near shutdown of the whole city because of the activities of two terrorists. Iran has already succeeded with laser enrichment in the laboratory. New varieties of enrichment are considered potentially dangerous because they can simplify the hardest aspect of making

6. "Statement of Hon. John Ensign," http://www.gpo.gov/fdsys/pkg/CHRG-110shrg80371/html/CHRG-110shrg80371.htm.

bomb-building fuel. Helen Caldicott had this to say about nuclear waste:

- The magnitude of the radiation generated in a nuclear power plant is almost beyond belief. The original uranium fuel that is subject to the fission process becomes one billion times more radioactive in the reactor core. A thousand megawatt nuclear power plant contains as much long-lived radiation as that produced by the explosion of one thousand Hiroshima-sized bombs.

- Every year, one-third of the now-intensely radioactive fuel rods must be removed from the reactor, because they are so contaminated with fission products that they hinder the efficiency of the electricity production.

- But they are also extremely thermally hot and must therefore be stored for thirty to sixty years in a heavily shielded building and continually cooled by air or water. If they are not continually cooled, the zirconium cladding of the rod could become so hot that it would spontaneously burn, releasing its radioactive inventory

- The construction and implementation processes involved in a gas-fired plant require only one-tenth of the energetic costs of a nuclear plant to produce the same amount of electricity.[7]

Kevin Kamps calls us to consider intergenerational equity, a concept also referred to by the US Department of Energy. He and Michael Keegan of Don't Waste Michigan have commented, "Electricity is but the fleeting byproduct of the Palisades nuclear reactor. The actual product is forever deadly radioactive waste."[8] Kamps further said, "It's a curse on all future generations, created by current generations just to turn on the lights—when we have many other options for doing so, that don't generate forever deadly poisons."[9]

7. See Caldicott, *Nuclear Power*, 14–15.
8. Keegan et al., "Public Comments," http://dwmi.homestead.com/.
9. Kevin Kamps, personal communication to author.

9

Scrawny-looking Dogs

The best remedy for those who are afraid, lonely, or unhappy is to go outside, somewhere where they can be quiet, alone with the heavens, nature and God.

—Anne Frank[1]

Scrawny-looking dogs roamed the desolate landscape surrounding the crippled Fukushima Daiichi reactors after the accident. Images of abandoned livestock and once-beloved pets left to fend for themselves in the wake of their owners' hasty departure were burned into our consciousness in the days after the nuclear power plant explosion.

Radiation from the crippled plant also killed sea life in unfathomable numbers in the days following the explosions at the Fukushima Daiichi power plant. But the cruelty to animals did not start with Fukushima Daiichi, nor was it unique to Fukushima

1. *Green Bible*, I–112.

Daiichi. It had already been happening to the sea turtles, mana-tees, dolphins, and other animals that are routinely taken up in nuclear cooling systems made up of thousands of pumps, valves, motors, and miles of electrical circuits. Human error, design flaws, and equipment malfunctions are common.

A million fish annually get chewed up by We Energies' Valley Plant built alongside the Menomonee River in Milwaukee. While this is not a nuclear plant, the principle remains the same (i.e., the fish are boiled).[2]

Add to that the large amount of aquatic life that is destroyed in the normal operation of the reactors long before the accident as animals with the misfortune of being in the wrong place are chewed up by the intake pipes and valves of the reactors.

God wants us to be in charge. We are to execute our steward-ship wisely and manage nature carefully.

The total disregard for human and even animal life under current nuclear policy can be compared to the depths of depravity perpetuated by the Nazis during the Holocaust.

We are not God. We are human beings who sin and need daily redemption. But there is hope for living in the Nuclear Age, even with all of its dangers and hazards. That hope is centered in the One who said of himself, "I am the Resurrection and the life" (John 11: 25–26).

Scrawny dogs and abandoned livestock roam the bleak coun-tryside, left to fend for themselves and eke out an existence in the area surrounding the crippled reactor. How many years must pass before people may once again farm the now highly toxic soil?

2. Cleaner Valley Coalition, "Valley's Outdated."

10

Fossil Fuel Follies

We must find ways to lessen the burden on Earth's resources, and we must encourage better stewardship of the planet so that all of us live in a clean and productive environment.

—Jimmy Carter[1]

The so-called "clean" energy from nuclear power plants relies heavily on "dirty" energy from fossil fuels. Both are problematic for our planet, as Helen Caldicott so eloquently explains:

> Most of the energy used to create nuclear energy—to mine uranium ore for fuel, to crush and mill the ore, to enrich the uranium, to create the concrete and steel for the reactor, and to store the thermally radioactively hot nuclear waste—comes from the consumption of fossil fuels, that is, coal or oil. When these materials are burned to produce energy, they form carbon dioxide (reflecting

1. Carter, "Challenges for Humanity."

63

coal and oil's origins in ancient trees and other organic carboniferous material laid down under the earth's crust millions of years ago). For each ton of carbon burned, 3.7 tons of carbon dioxide gas is added to the atmosphere, and this is the source of today's global warming.[2]

Here are some examples of the effects of global warming:

- The natural habitat of the polar bear is in serious decline, threatening the species' existence.

- Wildfires have increased in number and intensity.

- Tornadoes are deadlier and more destructive than ever.

- The hurricane season is growing longer, and more violent storms are expected as their reach increases.[3]

Global warming is a growing concern. As fossil fuels such as coal and gasoline are burned, they release carbon dioxide into the atmosphere. The carbon dioxide forms a reflective layer that locks in the heat radiating off the surface of the planet, much like what happens in a florist's greenhouse. That is why this phenomenon is often referred to as the "greenhouse effect." Indeed, "Carbon dioxide accounts for 50 percent of the global warming phenomenon, and other rare gases comprise the rest."[4]

British physicist Stephen Hawking also voiced his concerns about the survival of the human race: "We don't know where global warming will stop," he said. "But the worst case scenario is that Earth will become like its sister planet Venus with a temperature of 250 [Celsius] and raining sulfuric acid. The human race could not survive in those conditions."[5]

The hottest decade on record ever was the 1990s. Consider this anecdotal evidence: In the summer of 2000, the captain of a Russian icebreaker reported finding a mile-wide lake at the North Pole, something he had never encountered before—and for good

2. Caldicott, *Nuclear Power*, 4–6.

3. McKibben, "Climate Change."

4. Caldicott, *Nuclear Power*, 6.

5. Stephen Hawkin, qtd. in Paquette, "Five Lessons from Stephen Hawking."

reason. This was the first time the polar ice cap had melted in fifty million years! Moreover, scientists have discovered that the ice cover over the entire Arctic basin has thinned by 45 percent in the last forty years alone.

A study of twenty-six lakes and rivers in North America, Russia, Finland, and Japan by a researcher at the University of Wisconsin revealed further evidence of global warming. Using data from as long ago as 1846, this researcher discovered that the average first freezes on these bodies of water now occur 9.8 days later in the year, while the first thaw starts on average 8.7 days earlier now than 150 years ago.[6]

Scientists, working with data obtained at Mauna Loa Observatory in Hawaii, reported detecting record-high levels of carbon dioxide in the atmosphere in early 2004. They warned that it was accumulating at a record pace.[7]

The International Panel on Climate Change (IPCC), in a major report for the United Nations, warned that global warming threatens human life.[8] Here are some ways global warming will impact life as we know it on this planet:

- Rising ocean levels as the great polar ice caps melt could flood our coastal regions. During the past 100 years, the sea level along the US Atlantic coast has risen one foot already—its highest mark in the past five thousand years—and it is climbing as much as ten times faster than before. Many reactors, both in the US and worldwide, are located along sea coasts. During recent years' hot summers, reactors built alongside oceans and Great Lakes have been forced to shut down because the adjacent surface waters needed for cooling were too warm. This is especially true for riverside reactors. A reactor in Romania had to shut down several years ago when the

6. Mattmiller, "150-Year Global Ice Record," http://news.wisc.edu/5249.

7. See Keeling et al., "Atmospheric CO2 Records."

8. See Intergovernmental Panel on Climate Change, "Climate Change 2014."

river it depended on for cooling water dried up, leaving the cooling water intake pipe above the waterline![9]

- The southernmost part of Florida; the Mississippi River delta from Louisiana's Baton Rouge to the Gulf of Mexico; Venice, Italy; the Nile Delta, the Maldives; and Bangladesh are all areas of heavy population that would be inundated with rising waters. Florida Power and Light is actually proposing to build new reactors in a location that would surely be inundated by rising waters and was directly in the path of Hurricane Andrew.

- Rising sea levels would contaminate water supplies in coastal regions.

- The jet stream could change its path.

- The Midwest, the United States heartland that feeds the world, could become a desert if rainfall becomes less reliable.

- Cities in the west that depend on melting snow from nearby mountain ranges for their water—from Salt Lake City to Seattle and San Francisco to Los Angeles—could find these sources depleted if less snow were to fall due to warmer winter temperatures.

- The Gulf Stream, which warms Western Europe, could change directions, dooming that continent to cold summers and extremely harsh winters.

- Storms in many parts of the world are becoming more severe. For example, the area of water warm enough to produce hurricanes (80 degrees Fahrenheit) has already expanded by one-sixth over the past twenty years.

- In northern parts of Canada and Alaska, buildings constructed on the permafrost are sinking due to melting.

9. Bran, "Persistent Drought," http://www.theguardian.com/world/2011/dec/13/drought-in-romania-threatens-danube-power. See also Beyond Nuclear, "Fact Sheets," http://www.beyondnuclear.org/fact-sheets/.

- The expanding range of disease-carrying rodents and bugs such as mosquitoes and ticks would spread diseases like Malaria, encephalitis, and Lyme disease.

- More frequent hot spells would lead to an increase in heat-related deaths.

- The following crops could be imperiled:

  ◊ Chocolate: Cacao comes from places like Ghana and the Ivory Coast, where new temperature and rainfall patterns threaten cacao crops.

  ◊ Strawberries: Cool northern areas where strawberries thrive are likely to heat up.

  ◊ Coffee: Changes in rainfall, hurricanes, and crop depletion are threatening coffee production.

  ◊ Beer and Wine: Germany is suffering shortages of water needed to grow hops and barley for beer, while France's perfect climate for wine grapes may soon be lost.

  ◊ Trout and Salmon: Warm water may be good for beachgoers, but not for cold-water fish like trout and salmon.

  ◊ Maple Syrup: Acid rain, unpredictable weather, and insect infestations are threatening the delicate production of maple syrup.

The Kyoto Protocol was drafted in 1997 to reverse the causes for global warming. The protocol was signed by 160 nations. According to the protocol, industrialized nations are required to reduce their carbon dioxide emissions to an average of 5.2 percent below 1990 levels between 2008 and 2012. Unfortunately, few nations have taken the protocol seriously, and so global warming continues unabated.[10]

Today, the total human biomass is a hundred times greater as than any other large animal species ever to walk the earth. That growth has been aided by the use of fossil fuels as humans have learned to tap coal, oil, and natural gas. In fact, "Fossil-fuel

10. Shuster, *Beyond Fossil Fools*, 75.

combustion is adding billions of tons of carbon dioxide to the atmosphere each year, an inexorable escalation that must end soon if we are not to disrupt virtually every ecosystem and economy on the planet."[11]

Writer Bill McKibben always assumed it was "someone else's responsibility" to translate his ideas into activism. But a reporting trip to Bangladesh several years ago changed his mind.

The low-lying South Asian country is uniquely vulnerable to climate change, and while there, McKibben was stricken by dengue fever and used his recovery time to muse on the injustice of poor Bangladeshis suffering for the wealthy world's carbon habit. "If you try to measure the carbon footprint of Bangladesh, you'll barely get a number," he says. "There was this guilty part of me that said I had to do more."[12]

Apollo astronaut James Irwin wrote these words as he gazed back at Earth from the Apollo spacecraft en route to the moon:

The View from Space

The Earth reminded us of a Christmas tree ornament hanging in the blackness of space. As we got farther and farther away it diminished in size. Finally, it shrank to the size of a marble, the most beautiful marble you can imagine. That beautiful, warm, living object looked so fragile, so delicate, that if you touched it with a finger it would crumble and fall apart. Seeing this has to change a man, has to make a man appreciate the creation of God and the love of God.

—James Irwin, Apollo astronaut[13]

Faith in the Creator calls for each of us to do all we can to protect the environment by polluting less, conserving more,

---

11. Cothran, *Energy Alternatives*, 20.

12. McKibben, *Climate Change*.

13. Gaither, *Gaither's Dictionary*, 1789.

recycling regularly, and taking unpopular stands on these and other conservation issues. This is the bottom line: We must conserve energy, simplify our lifestyles, and clean up after ourselves. It is that simple—and that critical—for human life, given by a gracious God, to survive on this fragile "ornament hanging in the blackness of space."

11

Alternatives to Nuclear Power

We are losing the attitude of wonder, contemplation, listening to creation ... [When] we think and live in a horizontal manner, we have moved away from God, we no longer read His signs.

—Pope Francis[1]

Nuclear power plants cost in the range of $10 billion each when all the bills are paid. No one knows for sure. It would take a close look at the federal budget to sort through and decipher all the places where nuclear energy is listed.

Now let us consider some alternatives to nuclear energy by thinking outside the box. We will find that with increasing use of so-called "green" technology, electricity will become less expensive, and with good conservation, demand will actually reduce the

1. Pope Francis, qtd. in Vatican Radio, "Pope at Audience," http://en.radiovaticana.va/storico/2013/06/05/pope_at_audience_counter_a_culture_of_waste_with_solidarity/en1–698604.

need for any more nuclear power plants. Dare we dream of such a day?

We need to pursue strategies that use fewer non-renewable resources. For example, a motel under construction in Delavan, Wisconsin, will be entirely self-sufficient in producing its own energy. There are two types of alternative energy: resources that last forever, such as the sun; and the kind that are renewable, such as ethanol from corn. Let's take a look at eight different alternative energy sources.

Solar

The energy of the sun is harnessed by photovoltaic cells mounted on individual homes and businesses or clustered in solar farms. Solar panels are big and bulky and still too expensive to compete on the open market with conventional systems. Convergence Energy of Geneva Lake, Wisconsin, is building its own solar farm. Between the rows of rigid solar panels, a farmer has planted sunflower seeds that will be distilled into fuel to run the farm equipment. The panels were manufactured and installed by the local labor pool. The electricity produced will be plugged into the local electric power grid. This is an example of how alternatives can be pieced together so that down the road we won't need or want nuclear power plants.

Walgreens recently broke ground on America's first "zero energy" store in Evanston, Illinois. Using more than eight hundred solar panels, two wind turbines, and geothermal technology, the building will generate an estimated 256,000 kilowatt-hours of electricity per year, 28 percent more than the store will need. The company has already installed solar panels on 150 of its locations. The Fort Lauderdale, Florida, location combines extensive solar panels on the outside with power-saving technology on the inside.[2]

---

2. See the November 21, 2013 press release issues by Walgreens, "Net Zero Energy Retail Store."

Solar Thermal Concentration

A 500-megawatt electric facility is operating in California's Mojave Desert. It uses molten salt as an energy storage mechanism for nighttime or when the sun is not shining. Similar solar thermal concentration operations are already operating in Spain as well. There is tremendous energy potential, at large scale, in sunny places.[3]

Hydro

Wherever water falls, there is a potential site for hydroelectric power generation. Hydroelectric power plants have been around for a long time. We Energies, based in Milwaukee, Wisconsin, is currently exploring a partnership with the Canadian province of Manitoba for building a system of hydro dams and plants. The nation of Panama uses this source of energy for 70 percent of its energy needs. Brazil uses hydro for 80 percent. China has invested in the development of vast hydroelectric resources, most notably the Three Gorges Dam on the Yangtze River. The problem with such mega-hydro dams is that they are ecologically destructive. Millions of people have been displaced in China by the flooding, not to mention the submerged ecosystems. Micro-hydro power is much more sustainable because it works with the rivers instead of damming them.[4]

Tidal

The movement of ocean tides can be used to produce electricity. To be most effective, they need to tie into an existing power grid.

---

3. Nuclear Information and Rescue Service, "False Promises," 16.
4. Ibid, 18.

Wind

In parts of the country that have a steady supply of wind, there would be an inexhaustible supply of energy. Drivers heading south on I-39 from Rockford, Illinois, first see the twin cooling towers of Byron Nuclear Power Plant, which hopefully symbolize the "old school" method of power generation. A few miles further south, drivers encounter acre after acre of wind turbines that symbolize "new school" methods of power generation. Experts predict that wind will power 20 percent of the US energy needs by 2020. The technology is moving so quickly that it soon may supply a significant amount of our nation's insatiable appetite for electricity. In addition, wind turbines do not pollute, and they are aesthetically pleasing. Strategic locations can be chosen to avoid migratory bird flyways.[5]

Geothermal

This alternative energy source uses the earth's average temperature of approximately 60 degrees Fahrenheit to heat in the winter and cool in the summer.

Biogas

A byproduct of rotting garbage in our nation's overflowing landfills, biogas is mixed with coal or natural gas to generate electricity. Farm byproducts such as corncobs and stalks could be used to make biogas.

Oceanic Thermal Energy

The difference between the surface temperature of tropical waters and water found at depths of four thousand meters can also be used to generate electricity.

5. Ibid., 16.

Cogeneration

Since the 1960s, energy efficiency at conventional power plants (e.g., coal) in the United States has stagnated, with only 34 percent of energy generated as actual potential electricity. Cogeneration, or combined heat and power (CHP), finds uses for the remaining 66 percent that goes up the stacks as wasted heat. According to the US Department of Energy, "the energy lost in wasted heat from power generation in the U.S. is greater than the total energy use of Japan. CHP captures this waste energy and uses it to provide heating and cooling to factories and businesses, saving them money and improving the environment."[6] Already, cities like Tulsa, Oklahoma, have found that updating existing power plants to become more energy-efficient through cogeneration is better for their budgets, their citizens, and the environment. As the Nuclear Information and Rescue Service explains,

> Cogeneration already produces almost 9 percent of the power consumed in the US at a total efficiency nearly twice that of the rest of the country's power grid . . . Each dollar invested in electric efficiency in the US displaces nearly seven times as much carbon dioxide as a dollar invested in nuclear power and nuclear power saves as little as half as much carbon per dollar as wind power and cogeneration.[7]

Rather than building and maintaining nuclear energy facilities that put the health of both our families and our environment at risk, investing instead in cogeneration and similar energy-efficiency technologies is clearly the cost-effective and conscientious choice.

Conservation

It will not be necessary to build nuclear power plants in the first place if we all do some relatively easy tasks. We need to insulate

6. Office of Energy Efficiency and Renewable Energy, "Combined Heat and Power," 4.

7. Nuclear Information and Rescue Service, "False Promises," 19.

our homes and our places of business. We need to turn the thermostats down in the winter and up in the summer. Power use is already leveling off, and over the next ten years, it is expected to decline annually. Efficient use of energy-saving lightbulbs and new energy-efficient appliances are expected to improve even more during the next ten years. God intended the world to be used and inhabited, but we are to be careful how we use it to ensure that it not be gobbled up with little concern for generations yet unborn.

Alternative sources of electricity could be a real boon to third world countries if it would spare them from the horrendous cost of constructing nuclear plants. This is already happening in India, a country that ranks fifth in the world in wind energy production capacity. National hubris sometimes overwhelms common sense when it comes to nuclear power production. It is like a "keeping up with the Joneses" mentality played out on a global scale.

"Outrageous" is the best word to describe the arrangement reached during President Barack Obama's visit to India's Prime Minister in January 2015. Their agreement opens the door for US firms to sell nuclear reactors to India and allows those firms to avoid liability if a catastrophe were to unfold at an American-designed and -built reactor. As former NRC Commissioner Peter Bradford noted, trying to solve global warming by building nuclear power plants is like trying to solve global hunger by serving everyone caviar.[8]

What about the utility companies? There will be some adjustment in their corporate identities, but they will land on their feet. What they will leave us are the hulking cooling towers as an eyesore on our landscape forever. Even worse are the severely contaminated reactors and the high-level wastes with no safe place to go.

Alternatives cannot come soon enough. The United States' fleet of ninety-nine nuclear reactors is getting old. Reactors leak and show cracks. And make no mistake about this—the nuclear lobby is strong, well funded, and anxious to lead a "Nuclear Renaissance"—and it has a friend in the White House. The sooner we

8. See Bradford, "Costly and Dangerous."

can demonstrate success in the field of alternative energy sources, the better. If China develops all of its hydropower potential, and if the Chinese grid could be made to accommodate all of this power, then hydropower could replace all of China's coal-burning and other electricity-generating power plants at present consumption rates. However, even this staggering addition of electrical power would not be adequate to supply anticipated growth in China's population and economy. Any shortfall will likely be made up with nuclear energy, unfortunately. Hydropower from dams is subject to changes in climate, including variations in rainfall, ground and surface water levels, and glacial melt. Therefore, a backup plan is needed for low-water years.[9]

Over the next decade, experts expect residential power use to fall, reversing an upward trend that has been almost uninterrupted since Thomas Edison invented the modern lightbulb.[10] Fukushima Daiichi (on top of four decades of fierce grassroots antinuclear opposition) changed everything. In addition to shutting down eight reactors immediately, Germany agreed to close the remaining nine between now and 2022 and begin the transition to an economy run on low-carbon renewables. Germany leads Europe in wind power capacity and in 2011 doubled its solar capacity, which is now nearly as high as the rest of the world combined.[11] Germany is located far to the north, so imagine the solar potential in places like Florida and Arizona!

This is not a matter of *if* but of *when.* The longer we wait, the more costly and traumatic the transition to low-carbon renewables will be, and the greater the likelihood that the American economy will fall behind those of other countries that undertake the transition sooner.[12]

9. Shuster, *Beyond Fossil Fools*, 101.

10. Fahey, "Homes Use Less Power," 1.

11. Hockenos, *Nuclear Power*, 17.

12. Ibid., 22.

12

Call to Action

Let not any one pacify his conscience by the delusion that he can do no harm if he takes no part, and forms no opinion. Bad men need nothing more to compass their ends, than that good men should look on and do nothing.

—John Stuart Mill[1]

My brother and I were driving in Los Angles when he asked if there was anything he could show me. I said I always wanted to see the Hollywood sign. He looked at me with disbelief. "There," he said, pointing—and there it was, clearly visible in the distance. I felt dumb. But then I realized something else—that Southern California had done a terrific job of solving much of its smog problem. I thought back to the summer I worked in downtown LA. I made a daily commute on the Harbor Freeway, but I had never

---

1. Mill, "Inaugural Address," 24.

once seen that iconic sign because of the smog. My brother Bob, an elementary school principal, recalled days when the local schools had to deal with smog alerts and keep their kids indoors. All that is history now. In similar fashion, we will look back on these days of struggle to protect the planet from the dangers of nuclear power with a certain sense of having achieved a solid victory for God and for humanity.

Let's Look at the Record

- Nuclear power contributes to global warming, with all its attendant weather disasters. Nuclear power releases dangerous radioactive substances into the atmosphere and the waterways.
- Nuclear power leaves behind waste that lasts virtually forever.
- The nuclear power industry concentrates capital that could be put to better use.
- Nuclear power plants pose high risks for explosions and meltdowns at any time, causing catastrophic harm.
- The potential for subversive elements and disgruntled employees to capture radioactive materials remains largely unaddressed.
- The industry shows an alarming lack of preparation for nuclear accidents.
- Nuclear power plants are often built on poor sites, such as earthquake fault lines.

Five threads are coming together into a trend moving us toward confronting this serious threat to our environment.

1. *Economics.* One thread is the realization by operators of nuclear power plants that nuclear fission does not make economic sense. This conclusion was recently authenticated when the *Milwaukee Journal-Sentinel* reported that the owner of Wisconsin's Kewaunee nuclear plant would close the plant

in 2013. It simply cost too much to operate a nuclear power plant. "Operations and retrofits are economically challenging today because of growing supplies of natural gas."² A major reason for this decision was the fact that it costs less to generate electricity using natural gas than with nuclear generation—and this trend is likely to continue.

Nuclear power is simply not economical; it has only been kept alive by vast federal subsidies. On its own, nuclear power simply is not economical—and companies are beginning to see that fact, as evidenced by the growing use of wind and solar power. Could this be the beginning of the end for nuclear power? Could market forces finally catch up to nuclear power? Dr. Mark Cooper of Vermont Law School, an energy economist, says absolutely, yes. He identifies thirty-eight reactors nationwide that will likely be retired before their operating licenses expire and twelve more reactors that are at extreme risk for near-term, permanent shutdown.³

2. *Budget Crisis.* A second thread would be the looming crisis affecting the federal budget and many state budgets as well. If Congress truly wants to balance the budget, a place to begin might be the huge sums going to the Department of Energy and the Department of Defense for "weapons development." Perhaps I am naïve in trusting that the members of Congress can ignore the thousands of dollars pouring into their re-election campaigns and vote with common sense against the subsidies, favorable tax treatments, and loan guarantees Congress has historically lavished on the nuclear industry. Will Congress act in the best interests of our country? Can you think of a better target for budget-cutting than nuclear power? Billions of dollars could be saved or redirected toward uses that would give taxpayers a better return on their investment.

2. Learner, "Market Has Spoken," 11A.

3. Cooper, "Renaissance in Reverse," http://will.illinois.edu/nfs/RenaissanceinReverse7.18.2013.pdf.

3. *Global Warming.* A third thread moving us to confront nuclear power is best illustrated by Superstorm Sandy, which was responsible for widespread flooding; massive power outages, traffic tie-ups by air, automobile, and subway; over $50 billion in costs to homes, businesses, and infrastructure; and 121 deaths. Although the storm struck the densely populated northeastern United States, Sandy's wrath was felt as far west as Kenosha, Wisconsin. The disaster should be taken as a warning of the dangers of global warming. What if next time is worse? What if we get hit again? What if such natural disasters become a regular fact of life due to a shift in climatic patterns?[4]

4. *Nuclear Waste.* The next thread occurs when individual states lose their patience with the waste problem. They may set a moratorium on new construction until the waste problem is resolved. Perhaps they will establish blockades like California maintains to keep harmful invasive species from crossing state lines and threatening agricultural produce.

5. *Outrage.* The fifth and final thread is the one only you can provide: a sense of outrage at the risks placed on us by the nuclear power interest groups. This book has attempted to point out to the American people how wrong-headed the nuclear power industry has been and continues to be. We need to take to the streets in loud demonstrations against these demons and be prepared to undertake acts of civil disobedience if called upon. Like the spontaneous demonstrations that began in Ferguson, Missouri, and spread throughout the US following the deaths of unarmed black men at the hands of police officers, we need to join together in solidarity. Howard Zinn defines civil disobedience as "the deliberate violation of a law for a vital social purpose."[5] A good example would be the young people of the South of the 1950s and 60s who deliberately broke Jim Crow laws that attempted to separate the

4. Sheppard, "Under Water," 20.
5. Zinn, *Disobedience and Democracy*, 39.

races. The Revolutionary War was an act of civil disobedience writ large. And one of America's foundational documents, the Declaration of Independence, lays out the call to civil disobedience in bold and imaginative language.

Faith really matters. If we are to rid our world of these awful machines, then it will take acts of faith to make it happen. Faith is more than believing in a list of statements that we regard as true (the ecumenical creeds, for example). Faith comes alive when it is mixed with acts of courage and love. We, as people of God, can see our way through to a satisfactory resolution of the nuclear problem. Faith is a relationship with the living, loving God who places into our hands the care of the planet.

Conclusion

The nuclear power industry has done a disservice to the American people. Among its many absurdities is the fact that certain highly toxic wastes will be around for 240,000 years and beyond. Through our careless, mindless use of nuclear power, we have transgressed against God, against the creation, and against our children's world. The time has come to pull the plug on nuclear power.

Bibliography

Abraham, Spenser, and William Tucker. *Lights Out! 10 Myths about (and Teal Solutions to) America's Energy Crisis.* New York: St. Martin's, 2010.

Aeschliman, Gordon. "Loving the Earth Is Loving the Poor." *The Green Bible: Understand the Bible's Powerful Message for the Earth (NRSV),* foreword by Desmond Tutu, 1:1–94. San Francisco: HarperOne, 2008.

Baynton, Chuck. "The Perils of Nuclear Power." *Milwaukee Journal Sentinel,* June 22, 2011, http://www.jsonline.com/news/opinion/124386603.html.

Beckmann, David. *Exodus from Hunger: We Are Called to Change the Politics of Hunger.* Louisville: Westminster John Knox, 2010.

Benen, Steve, "The Underlying Social Contract." *Washington Monthly,* September 21, 2011. http://www.washingtonmonthly.com/political-animal/2011_09/the_underlying_social_contract032342.php.

Beyond Nuclear. "Dirty, Dangerous and Expensive: The Verdict Is in on Nuclear Power." Takoma Park, MD, November 2009. Pamphlet. http://static1.1.sqspcdn.com/static/f/356082/6186633/1268920948460/BNDDE2009-new.pdf?token=nXGA1XH0UT6sg25fHATKjYN9sFg%3D.

———. "Fact Sheets." http://www.beyondnuclear.org/fact-sheets/.

———. "Fukushima 4 Years On." *The Thunderbird* 3 (2015). http://static1.1.sqspcdn.com/static/f/356082/26029242/1425990548673/OnLine_Thunderbird_BeyondNuclear_March2015.pdf?token=Hcy4eg2%2BLdKqQa6mKMgRW2%2FCVNc%3D.

———. "The Lethal Legacy of the Atomic Age 1942–2012–Infinity." Takoma Park, MD, January 2012. Pamphlet. http://static1.1.sqspcdn.com/static/f/356082/16107103/1326916854883/Waste_70YearsHigh_2012.pdf?token=Vzbvud4NaGMUA4l%2FEwxSbUBUn8g%3D.

———. "NRC Denies Modest Post-Fukushima Emergency Response Recommendations." April 30, 2014. http://www.beyondnuclear.org/nuclear-power/2014/4/9/nrc-denies-modest-post-fukushima-emergency-response-recommen.html.

Bibliography

————. "Nuclear Power and Children." Takoma Park, MD, March 2014. Pamphlet.
   http://static1.1.sqspcdn.com/static/f/356082/24565692/1395264688257/
   NuclearPower_and_Children_BN_March2014.pdf?token=2LlUToRNB
   %2FPzXPobupKp3H%2BFOMo%3D.

————. "Updated! Routine Radioactive Releases from U.S. Nuclear Power Plants."
   Takoma Park, MD, December 2012 (updated November 2013). Pamphlet.
   http://static1.1.sqspcdn.com/static/f/356082/23975081/1385586922000/
   Routine+Releases+from+U.S.+Nuclear+Power+Plants_November_2013.
   pdf?token=DVso%2BXEBZu5nD%2F1HEwIuAfjV%2F%2BI%3D.

Borg, Marcus J. *Meeting Jesus Again for the First Time: The Historical Jesus and
   the Heart of Contemporary Faith*. San Francisco: Harper Collins, 1995.

————. *Reading the Bible Again for the First Time: Taking the Bible Seriously but
   Not Literally*. New York: Harper Collins, 2001.

Bradford, Peter A. "Should the World Increase Its Reliance on Nuclear
   Energy? No: It Is Costly and Dangerous." *The Wall Street Journal*.
   October 8, 2012. http://www.wsj.com/news/articles/SB10000
   872396390443995604578001973671148176?mod=WSJ_hpp_
   LEFTTopStories&mg=reno64-wsj&url=http%3A%2F%2Fonline.wsj.co
   m%2Farticle%2FSB10000872396390443995604578001973671148176.
   html%3Fmod%3DWSJ_hpp_LEFTTopStories.

Bran, Mirel. "Persistent Drought in Romania Threatens Danube's Power." *The
   Guardian*. December 13, 2011. http://www.theguardian.com/world/2011/
   dec/13/drought-in-romania-threatens-danube-power. This only refers to
   the shutdown of that reactor in Romania.

Bread for the World Institute. "About Hunger: Who Experiences Hunger."
   http://www.bread.org/who-experiences-hunger.

Brueggemann, Walter. "The Liturgy of Abundance, the Myth of Scarcity:
   Consumerism and Religious Life." *Generous Steward Resources*.http://
   www.thegeneroussteward.com/uploads/The_Liturgy_of_Abundance.pdf.

Caldicott, Helen. *Nuclear Power Is Not the Answer*. New York: New Press, 2006.

Carroll, Anthony. "AARP Survey: Opinions of Likely and Registered Voters in
   Iowa on Advance Ratemaking Legislation," *AARP*. May 23, 2011. http://
   assets.aarp.org/rgcenter/general/iowa-voters-advance-ratemaking-
   legislation.pdf.

Carter, Jimmy. "Challenges for Humanity: A Beginning." *National Geographic
   Magazine*, February 1, 2002.

Cleaner Valley Coalition. "Valley's Outdated Technology Is Killing Aquatic
   Wildlife." *Cleaner Milwaukee Coalition*. August 2, 2012. http://
   cleanermilwaukeecoalition.org/2012/08/02/valleys-outdated-technology-
   is-killing-aquatic-wildlife/.

Cooper, Mark. "Renaissance in Reverse: Competition Pushes Aging US Nuclear
   Reactors to the Brink of Economic Abandonment." July 18, 2013. http://
   will.illinois.edu/nfs/RenaissanceinReverse7.18.2013.pdf.

Cothran, Helen. *Energy Alternatives: Opposing Viewpoints*. San Diego:
   Greenhaven, 2002.

Bibliography

Crossan, John Dominic. *Jesus: A Revolutionary Biography*. San Francisco: Harper Collins, 1993.

Drey, Kay. "Nuclear Power's Dirty Secret." In *Viewpoint: A Forum on Energy and Environmental Issues*, pamphlet. Safe Energy Communications Council, 1990.

Fahey, Jonathan. "Homes Use Less Power." *Milwaukee-Wisconsin Journal Sentinel*, December 30, 2013. http://www.jsonline.com/business/homes-use-less-power-b99174301z1-238178951.html.

Gaither, Carl C., and Alma E. Cavazos-Gaither, eds. *Gaither's Dictionary of Scientific Quotations*. 2nd ed. New York: Springer, 2012.

The Green Bible: Understanding the Bible's Powerful Message for the Earth [NRSV]. New York: Harper Collins, 2008.

Grossman, Karl. "The NRC's Latest Crazy Idea: An 80-Year License to Kill?" *Counter Punch*, June 4, 2012, http://www.karlgrossman.com/Articles. html#The NRC's Latest Crazy Idea.

Grunwald, Michael. "The Real Cost of U.S. Nuclear Power." *Time Magazine*, March 28, 2011. http://content.time.com/time/magazine/article/0,9171,2059603-2,00.html.

Gugel, John. *Messiah*. St. Louis: Creative Communications for the Parish, 2003.

Hockenos, Paul. "Nuclear Power? Germany Says 'Nein Danke.'" *The Nation*, March 19, 2012. http://www.thenation.com/article/166520/nuclear-power-germany-says-nein-danke.

Hoviss, Daniel. "Iitate Village–Sister Town to Putney VT: Residents Leave Japan's 'Most Beautiful Village' Amidst Crisis." June 2011. http://www.brattleboro.net/action-center/actions/iitate-village-sister-town-to-putney-vt/.

Huber, Elaine. "We Survived 3 Mile Island." In *Power for Living: The First Step*, by Arthur DeMoss. Garland, TX: American Tract Society: March 30, 1980.

Intergovernmental Panel on Climate Change [IPCC]. "Climate Change 2014: Synthesis Report." Contribution of Working Groups I, II, and III to the Fifth Assessment Report of the Intergovernmental Panel on Climate Change, edited by the Core Writing Team, R.K. Pachauri, and L.A. Meyer. Geneva: IPCC, 2014. https://www.ipcc.ch/pdf/assessment-report/ar5/syr/SYR_AR5_FINAL_full.pdf.

Keegan, Michael J. "Public Comments re: Environmental Impact Statement re: Proposed 20 Year Extension of the Operating License for the Palisades Nuclear Power Plant." *Don't Waste Michigan*. Email to US Nuclear Regulatory Commission submitted electronically to PalisadesEIS@nrc.gov on August 22, 2005. http://dwmi.homestead.com/.

Keeling, R. F., et al. "Atmospheric CO2 Records from Sites in the SIO Air Sampling Network. In *Trends: A Compendium of Data on Global Change*. Oak Ridge, TN: Carbon Dioxide Information Analysis Center, Oak Ridge National Laboratory, US Department of Energy, 2009. DOI: 10.3334/CDIAC/atg.035. http://cdiac.ornl.gov/ftp/trends/co2/maunaloa.co2.

Bibliography

King, Martin Luther, Jr. "I've Been to the Mountaintop." April 3, 1968. *Stanford University Martin Luther King, Jr. Research and Education Institute*. http:// kingencyclopedia.stanford.edu/encyclopedia/encyclopedia/enc_ive_ been_to_the_mountaintop_3_april_1968/.

King, Martin Luther, Jr., and Coretta Scott King. *The Words of Martin Luther King, Jr.* 2nd ed. New York: Newmarket, 2008.

Küng, Hans. *On Being a Christian*. Garden City, NY: Doubleday, 1976.

Learner, Howard A. "Market Has Spoken in Kewaunee Shutdown." *Milwaukee Journal Sentinel*, October 30, 2012.

Mattmiller, Brian. "150-Year Global Ice Record Reveals Major Warming Trend." University of Wisconsin-Madison News. September 7, 2000. http://news. wisc.edu/5249.

McKibben, Bill. "Climate Change: Just the Facts." *Sojourners Magazine*, April 2011.

Mill, John Stuart. "Inaugural Address: Delivered to the University of St. Andrews, Feb. 1st, 1867." London: Longmans, Green, Reader & Dyer, 1867. http://babel.hathitrust.org/cgi/pt?id=hvd.32044018937722;view=1 up;seq=30.

National Commission on Terrorist Attacks upon the United States. "The 9/11 Commission Report." http://govinfo.library.unt.edu/911/ report/911Report.pdf.

Nuclear Information and Rescue Service [NIRS]. "False Promises: Debunking Nuclear Industry Propaganda." Takoma Park, MD: NIRS, 2008. http:// www.nirs.org/falsepromises.pdf.

Office of Energy Efficiency and Renewable Energy. "Combined Heat and Power: A Clean Energy Solution." *US Department of Energy and US Environmental Protection Agency*. August 2012. https://www1.eere.energy. gov/manufacturing/distributedenergy/pdfs/chp_clean_energy_solution. pdf.

Osnos, Evan. "The Fallout. Seven Months Later: Japan's Nuclear Predicament." *The New Yorker*, October 17, 2011.

Paquette, Danielle. "Five Lessons from Stephen Hawking." *The Washington Post*. November 10, 2014. https://www.washingtonpost.com/news/storyline/ wp/2014/11/10/five-climate-lessons-from-stephen-hawking/.

Pope Francis. "A Heartless Cult of Money." *Sojourners Magazine*, September– October 2013.

Reader, Mark, et al., eds. *Atom's Eve: Ending the Nuclear Age, An Anthology*. New York: McGraw-Hill, 1980.

Sheppard, Kate. "Under Water: Flood, Rebuild, Repeat." *Mother Jones*, July- August 2013.

Shuster, Joseph. *Beyond Fossil Fools: The Roadmap to Energy Independence by 2040*. Edina, MN: Beaver's Pond, 2008.

Spong, John Shelby. *Rescuing the Bible from Fundamentalism: A Bishop Rethinks the Meaning of Scripture*. San Francisco: HarperCollins, 1992.

Bibliography

"Statement of Hon. John Ensign, U.S. Senator from Nevada." In "Safety and Security of Spent Nuclear Fuel Transportation," S. Hrg. 110–1222 before the Committee on Commerce, Science, and Transportation, September 24, 2008. Washington, DC: US Government Printing Office, 2013. http://www.gpo.gov/fdsys/pkg/CHRG-110shrg80371/html/CHRG-110shrg80371.htm.

Stephenson, Robin. "We Are Takers: A Prayer by Walter Brueggemann." November 29, 2011. http://blog.bread.org/2011/11/we-are-takers-a-prayer-by-walter-brueggemann.html.

"Tank Storing Radioactive Waste Leaking in Washington." *CNN*. February 16, 2011. http://www.cnn.com/2013/02/15/us/washington-tank-leak/.

Vatican Radio. "Pope at Audience: Counter a Culture of Waste with Solidarity." UN World Environment Day address given at Saint Peter's square, June 5, 2013. http://en.radiovaticana.va/storico/2013/06/05/pope_at_audience_counter_a_culture_of_waste_with_solidarity/en1–698604.

Walgreens. "Walgreens Debuts Nation's First Net Zero Energy Retail Store in Evanston, Ill." Edited by Emily Hartwig. November 21, 2013. http://news.walgreens.com/index.cfm.

Zinn, Howard. *Disobedience and Democracy: Nine Fallacies on Law and Order.* New York: Vintage, 1968.

www.ingramcontent.com/pod-product-compliance
Lightning Source LLC
Chambersburg PA
CBHW060418090426
42734CB00011B/2356